T0147155

FINDING YOUR PACE

Bridging the Gap Between Apathy
and Being All God Called You to be

Romney J. Ruder

WESTBOW
PRESS®
A DIVISION OF THOMAS NELSON
& ZONDERVAN

WestBow Press books may be ordered through booksellers or by contacting:

WestBow Press
A Division of Thomas Nelson & Zondervan
1663 Liberty Drive
Bloomington, IN 47403
www.westbowpress.com
844-714-3454

ISBN: 978-1-6642-8121-9 (sc)
ISBN: 978-1-6642-8122-6 (hc)
ISBN: 978-1-6642-8120-2 (e)

Library of Congress Control Number: 2022919101

Print information available on the last page.

WestBow Press rev. date: 11/10/2022

Contents

Acknowledgements

For my wife Amy who has been my best friend and partner for over 25 years. She has run the race beside me regardless of the obstacles.

To my sons and daughter in-law, who are the arrows of my life (Psalm 127:4) and helped set a pace during this project by reaching for the stars in their own endeavors. God is doing great things with each of you and I am excited to watch it happen.

Foreword

It has been a great privilege for me to join hands with Lifeline Global Ministries. I'll never forget my first experience at Angola State Prison when a large group of men was honored for completing the yearlong, Malachi Dads program. I was also deeply honored to present my *Life Essentials Study Bible* to each graduate and be able to spend some time training them to use it. Frankly, it was a life-changing experience.

Since then, the opportunities have only multiplied. From Florida to California and beyond, men and women in a multitude of prisons are not only being redeemed through their faith in Jesus Christ, but they are growing and maturing in Christ because of Lifeline Global Ministries.

You'll learn more about this ministry in *Finding Your Pace* but even more significant, you'll learn what it really means to enter and follow the narrow path that leads to life eternal. You will also immensely enjoy Romney's athletic metaphors and similar biblical examples. The Apostle Paul loved to illustrate biblical truth with these illustrations even when facing death. Thus, he wrote, "I have fought the good fight, I have finished the race, I have kept the faith" (2 Timothy 4:7).

Dr. Gene A. Getz

Professor, Pastor, Author

Introduction

It is not the critic who counts; not the man who points out how the strong man stumbles, or where the doer of deeds could have done them better. The credit belongs to the man who is actually in the arena, whose face is marred by dust and sweat and blood; who strives valiantly; who errs, who comes short again and again, because there is no effort without error and shortcoming; but who does actually strive to do the deeds; who knows great enthusiasms, the great devotions; who spends himself in a worthy cause; who at the best knows in the end the triumph of high achievement, and who at the worst, if he fails, at least fails while daring greatly, so that his place shall never be with those cold and timid souls who neither know victory nor defeat.
Theodore Roosevelt, Citizenship in a Republic

The cold bit through my gear as I tried to move as much as possible, wondering if I was a little crazy for being out that early on a Labor Day weekend in freezing Montreal, Canada. My wife, Amy, and I waited on a bridge over the St. Lawrence River. It felt like the starting gun to begin the Montreal Half-marathon would never go off. I was trying to remember how I had come up with this nutty idea. Like many American males, I have flitted in and out of athletic ventures; the year before was my foray into short triathlons. That winter, I decided to do something nice for my wife's upcoming birthday. She had never been to Canada, and Montreal is a great place to get away for an extended weekend, so that is where I chose.

As a good husband should, I wanted to make sure we had a full itinerary, as my wife likes to stay active. When I saw the Montreal Marathon was being held the same weekend, it was a no-brainer. (Except I now wondered if the no-brain part was literal.)

This trip was unique from the various highs and lows I experienced in doing this. My wife was over the moon when I announced the trip and I enjoyed all kinds of love and affection. Then I hit her with, "Surprise! We're going to run in a marathon too!"

My wife's jaw dropped and she stared at me with a *We are going to do what?* look.

I cleared my throat, tugged at my t-shirt collar, and explained that it would be *awesome.* She wasn't convinced.

Soon enough, the excitement of the trip overcame the reluctance toward the marathon, and before long we were both ready to start training. The first reality check for me was being informed that our mere tennis shoes would never be suitable for a race of this magnitude. My wife decreed that we had to go to the running shoe store to be fitted for gazillion-dollar pairs that you would have thought were custom-made for each of us. Then, for anyone who has ever purchased a pair of gazillion-dollar running shoes, you know that ordinary socks will never do, so the grinning store associate dropped several pairs of zillion-dollar socks into the bag to accompany our new shoes.

We had nine months to prepare so we began by researching heavily regarding which training program would be best for us. At the time, we were living in the Midwest, which comes with its ample share of cold and snow. We had the motivation but the cold and snow threw a monkey wrench into our training schedule. By the first signs of spring, we had lost our training log and were blessed to get in a good daily walk. When summer arrived, I knew we were in trouble.

The marathon had a time limit so the question arose of how we would complete 26.2 miles under the time limit with basically no training. Did we go for a *Hail Mary* and ramp up our training during the last few weeks, kicking ourselves into gear to make sure we were ready? Of course not. I simply made a call to the registration office, explained the situation, and had them switch us to the half marathon.

This made us feel much better.

We now had a reduced goal that was more manageable. Plus we still had a decent amount of time to train for this shorter event, right? Wrong. Our ministry quickly got the better of us. Summer was definitely not the season to prepare for this endeavor. Between summer camps, speaking engagements, discipleship, church groups, and kids' activities, we were swamped. Needless to say, we got barely any training in.

So there we were, in the early morning freezing on a bridge on the far side of Canada with a long race before us. To make matters worse, I made the mistake of thinking they were going to serve us a light breakfast, so I told Amy not to eat anything at the hotel. The words of my football coach rang out in my ears, "A hungry dog hunts best," but Amy was about ready to gnaw my arm off.

Thousands of people huddled together with us on that bridge, trying desperately to somehow shield ourselves from the cutting wind that blew off the river. Amy occasionally cast me a glance that said, *This was not your brightest idea!* I agreed. We could have been enjoying fresh pastries at one of the downtown bistros. Instead, we were waiting to start a race I wasn't even sure we could finish.

As I waited for that blasted gun to go off, I tried to get myself pumped up for the undertaking. One of those techno dance numbers was being pounded into the crowd and it was so loud the bass reverberated through my brain. *Thump, thump, thump, thump!* I had to get myself focused so I began to think of any famous runners I knew. I didn't know any. Hmmm. Then I remembered the apostle Paul. I love Paul. Maybe it is because I am a guy or maybe because I grew up on sports and competition, but he uses language that really gets me going. I look at Paul as just a no-nonsense guy; what you see is what you get with Paul. Sure, he had some rough edges, but he wasn't consumed with himself. Rather, he was focused on the life of Christ and fulfilling all the Lord had in store for him.

It was Paul who, as he was summarizing his life's work, tells us in 2 Timothy 4:7, "I have fought the good fight, I have finished the race, I have kept the faith." (It is hard for me to hear these words without picturing Al Pacino in the movie *Scent of a Woman* shouting "Hoooaaah!" Or hearing Tim "The Tool Man" Taylor in the show *Home Improvement* barking, "Aooourrrgh! Aooouuurrgh!")

Paul's words strengthened me. I mean, if Paul finished the race, if he fought the good fight, if he kept the faith until the end despite all the torture he went through, well then I could persevere through this little race as well. After all, Paul was just a man as I was a man. Granted, he did witness God and was named an apostle, but in the end, he was made of flesh and blood just like I am.

With the race starting, I knew I may have to overcome some pain and suffering of my own. By that point, however, one thing was for certain ... I was going to see this race through to the end.

Finally, the starting gun went off and the hordes crawled off the bridge and spread out onto the road. Soon into mile one, I winked at Amy but it was to cover the fact that I realized it was going to be a long, grinding, endeavor. Truth be known there is not a lot to do in a race like this. For a short while, you enjoy seeing the sites, and there are certain areas where the spectators' shouts of support really get you going. As far as activity goes, though, you just make sure you stay upright and keep your legs moving.

Now I have many friends who run for a lot of different reasons. Some just enjoy the feel of running—the endorphins kicking in, the wind blowing in their hair, being outside. I do not fall into that group. I was not at a point where it was about the experience; it was just about getting to the end while limiting the damage to my body.

By mile two I was already huffing and puffing too heavily to talk to my wife so I decided to let my mind explore a little further regarding the scripture I had used to get me motivated. In 2 Timothy, Paul is obviously not talking about running a literal 5K or some marathon, but instead, he was speaking about the proverbial race of life. As I pondered that context, I marveled at the apostle. What a life Paul led. By all worldly standards there was a guy who was at the top of his game; he was highly educated, he ran with the right crowd (the Pharisees), he came from a good lineage (he was a Benjamite, and a Roman Citizen), and not to mention he had a high profile job persecuting those troublemaking Christians who upset both Israel and Rome's apple carts.

Obviously, Paul had a divine course correction, but he clearly went all in on whatever he was tasked with, whether pre-salvation or post. Paul completed his races; he saw them through to the end. Then a question flickered through my mind ... *But at what pace did he accomplish it?* As I approached mile three, I continued to contemplate this idea.

As the miles passed, and I went deeper and deeper into the race metaphor, I began to see that Paul's race and the physical race I was engaged in, paralleled what was happening in the modern-day Church. I mean, think about it. When it comes to following Jesus Christ, what percentage of your church would you indicate are "in the race" so to speak? That is, how many actively reflect the kind of life that our Savior lived? How many are running the type of race Paul is speaking of? If you said ten percent of the church is "on fire" I would say that this is probably average. If your body has twenty-five percent of the members active, it would appear that you are doing great. If you say any more than twenty-five percent are running their race diligently though, I am inclined to believe you are just fooling yourselves.

I'll admit I am not drawing conclusions from any sources of measured data. Rather, I am speaking from experience as a man who has been involved with many churches and is speaking from the heart. I would be the first to say it is not my responsibility to determine whether a person is actively engaged in following the leadership and submitted to the lordship of Christ. With over half of the United States population referring to themselves as Christians, however, I have to question what is God telling us in Matthew 7:14 when He says, "For the gate is narrow and the way is hard that leads to life, and those who find it are few" (ESV). I know what you may be thinking because I have had the same thought. Jesus certainly can't be referring to us ... He must be referring to those people on the other side of town who live a lifestyle that couldn't be discussed at Sunday morning worship.

You know the lifestyle I am talking about. It is the lifestyle that many of us, myself included, have lived ourselves. If we are going to take a good, soul-searching look at ourselves, many of us are probably still living these lifestyles now. Maybe we are not robbing liquor stores, but we are still under-reporting our taxes. Although we are not lying to a grand jury, we are willing to use a sick day for an extra day of vacation. We obediently offer our tithe every week, but when forced between giving someone in need a meal and buying the next five-dollar cup of coffee, the coffee always wins.

Better yet, we like to believe Jesus is talking about those people on the other side of the world who have never heard of Christ, or who have succumbed to a false religion. Yet, how quickly we lose sight of what is truth in the gospel of our own minds. In the modern-day Church, we are guilty of developing and idolizing our own lifestyles and kingdoms; creating our own way to the salvation we believe we need. Much of this is conformed to the patterns of this world that Romans 12 tells us so plainly we are to reject. When you look at today's Church, can we honestly say we have seen a transformation from renewed minds?

As I rounded a large bend, I wondered *Who exactly is God talking to here in this passage of Matthew?* If we take an honest look at the passage as it is, Jesus is talking directly to *me*; He is talking to *you*; He is talking to the Church. Listen to what Christ says in Luke 13: 22-30 (NIV):

> [22] Then Jesus went through the towns and villages, teaching as he made his way to Jerusalem. [23] Someone asked him, "Lord, are only a few people going to be saved?" He said to them, [24] "Make every effort to enter through the narrow door, because many, I tell you, will try to enter and will not be able to. [25] Once the owner of the house gets up and closes the door, you will stand outside knocking and pleading, 'Sir, open the door for us.' "But he will answer, 'I don't know you or where you come from.' [26] "Then you will say, 'We ate and drank with you, and you taught in our streets.' [27] "But he will reply, 'I don't know you or where you come from. Away from me, all you evildoers!' [28] "There will be weeping there, and gnashing of teeth, when you see Abraham, Isaac and Jacob and all the prophets in the kingdom of God, but you yourselves thrown out. [29] People will come from east and west and north and south, and will take their places at the feast in the kingdom of God. [30] Indeed there are those who are last who will be first, and first who will be last."

Does this passage trouble you some? It sure does me. How do we ensure that we stay on the straight and narrow path? Scripture provides clear instructions in many places regarding the path we are to take. In Ecclesiastes, we are instructed specifically about our duty as children of God. It says we are to fear God and keep his commandments (Ecclesiastes 12:13) but we know that Christ went even farther than this. Christ turned the world of leadership upside down as He told us that in order to be first, we must first be last. He epitomized servant leadership for us. His specific instruction comes in Matthew 28:19 (NIV) which we all know so well: "Therefore, go and make disciples of all nations ..."

Notice Jesus isn't specifically speaking to one person or another. In this verse, Jesus is speaking to *all* of us, yet somehow we read this and infer our own meaning. If, for example, my wife takes the spiritual gifts class and her assessment indicates she is an evangelist, we are tempted to believe that only she and other evangelists must go out and spread the good news. Everyone else is off the hook. The rest of us can feel free to take comfort in our salvation, and all we need to do is participate in a Sunday school class or two and a service on the weekends.

No, Christ didn't intend for this to be directed at certain believers; He means it to be a way of life for all who claim to be His followers. Notice the first word: "GO!" It doesn't require much of a definition. Much like a starting gun, or a race announcer shouting, "Ready ... Set ... GO!" We are *all* meant to shoot off our starting blocks and start *going*. Going into our neighborhood with the gospel, going into our city's downtown metro, going into war-torn places where people need urgent care, going anywhere and everywhere the Lord calls us.

You wouldn't stop at a stoplight when it is green, would you? This is what Paul is referring to when he describes the race. Christ wants us to get in the race. He has called you to be on His team. Nobody on God's team gets to just wear the Lettermen's jacket to show off that they made the team. God expects you to be running *for the entire race*.

I was stunned to look up and see the finish line on the horizon. We had just about made it. While I was focused on Jesus I didn't even feel the burning in my legs. I grinned and looked over at

Amy. Her eyes instantly told me she knew I was deep in thought and she had let me be ... but once we crossed that finish line, if I didn't get her to one of Montreal's exquisite breakfast spots promptly, she literally *would* gnaw off my arm.

ONE

Get in the Race

I'm in the race
moving on to you Father
No more turning back
I'm in the race to my destiny
Until I see you my redeemer,
until I see the Man who died for me
I will never lose my way
'cause I'm in the race to my destiny[1]

WOULD YOU AGREE THAT THE TOUGHEST PART OF ANY RACE IS finding the motivation to begin? The reasons to *not* run far outweigh the reasons *to* run. I guess in some cases laziness could be a factor, but getting into a race is often just one more thing added to the already-full plate of life. Complacency could be another reason—there is the old saying that if it ain't broke, don't fix it. Then we have to consider that committing to a race usually requires we shake up a routine we have worked long and hard to keep consistent. There are many reasons, valid and invalid, to excuse us from running but I think the one at the very top of my list is common to many people: *the fear of failure.*

---

[1] Mwai, Paul. 2013. *Racing Up.* Africha Entertainment Limited.

I have never been one of those people who can just participate for the love of the sport. I wish I could be this way, but it is simply not the way that God designed me. I just don't enjoy running that much ... however ... the competitive part of me wants to excel. I don't need to win the race, mind you. I don't necessarily compete against others to be the best, rather, it is an internal competition stemming from the fact that I know what I have accomplished in the past or what I should be capable of.

In life, much as in running, so many times the easiest way to not live up to my potential (and seriously disappoint myself) is by never getting started at all. All of us have been there at one time or another, but for some reason, we are captive to the idea that if we cannot be good at it instantly, there is no reason to even try it.

I know it sounds ludicrous that we might have this notion of instant excellence, especially if we have gone some time without practice or participation. We find ourselves out of shape and out of practice and yet we feel like we are supposed to be right back where we left off. Even if it is an endeavor we have never tried before, we usually have the same mindset.

I used to live on the west coast, and that was how I approached surfing. I have quite a few friends who would go out regularly and they constantly invited me along. I always resisted. Don't get me wrong, it looked like total fun; these guys had a blast riding the tiniest of waves. They talked about the bliss of being on the water and being in tune with the Holy Spirit. We sometimes laughed that when Genesis says the Spirit of God was hovering above the water He was doing so on a surfboard. Now I love being in the water and I love the beach so you would think the sport would be perfect for me. Yet, I have hesitated because I didn't know how to do it and it is more than a little tricky to get started.

The one foray I made into surfing resulted in an hour of spending more time with the board riding me instead of me riding the surfboard. My two boys would go out and make it look really simple, though. They hopped right up and rode whatever wave came along. Not only could I not get up but I couldn't even balance on the board lying down. I just kept wobbling in the water and flipping over one side. Now why would I want to continue wasting my efforts to see how fast I can drink in the ocean? *I did it because I wanted to experience communion with the Lord that I felt was out there on the water.* I knew that in order to succeed at this it would take effort and practice on my part. It would definitely not happen overnight. One thing was certain—if I did not put in the effort to even get in the water, it would *never* happen.

In the same way, God knows we need to make an effort to learn the race of serving Him.

In Dietrich Bonhoeffer's, *The Cost of Discipleship*[2], I love his courage to define "cheap grace" as what it really is: nothingness. Bonhoeffer describes many Christians whose only obedience to follow Christ is showing up to service on (most) Sundays. While I don't want to put words in his mouth, I believe Bonhoeffer is describing genuine faith contrasted with a mere "verbal" faith—a mental ascent to faith in which we say we believe but we have no willingness to step out of the world and take up our cross in obedience to the One who saved us. How can we learn to run if we won't start? Although Bonhoeffer was referring to the state of the Church in the last century, one could safely argue that not much has changed in this day and age. It honestly might even be worse.

I believe too many people (myself included), who refer to themselves as Christians, are missing the mark. Our focus is pulled to the busyness of life instead of our respective individual and specific callings, and unfortunately, this is exactly what the enemy desires. If he can accomplish his goal of stealing our attention away from Jesus Christ he can keep us in a perpetual delusion of believing we're running while we're still on the bench.

---

[2] Bonhoeffer, Dietrich. *The Cost of Discipleship.* Touchstone; 1st edition Paperback, September 1, 1995.

If he can fill our heads and time with things that are secondary, even if they are necessary, we will miss Christ's call. I am the chief offender as Paul says (1 Timothy 1:15) but I am jumping into my race with this book.

I earnestly pray the Church sees the warning signs and that we can make the proper adjustments. Is the world getting crazier and crazier because Christians are sitting on the sidelines believing they're running? What would happen if we all actually started running? Maybe there would be a revival led by authentic disciples of Christ the likes of which this world has never seen.

Look what it says in Jeremiah 5:27-29:

> [27] Like a cage full of birds, their houses are full of deceit; therefore they have become great and rich; [28] they have grown fat and sleek. They know no bounds in deeds of evil; they judge not with justice the cause of the fatherless, to make it prosper, and they do not defend the rights of the needy. [29] Shall I not punish them for these things? declares the Lord, and shall I not avenge myself on a nation such as this?"

It sure sounds like the prophet is describing American Christianity, doesn't it? We are the richest country in the world yet we still fall severely short of addressing issues of true social justice, especially as it applies to those lacking fathers. Additionally, the Church has allowed the government to take the lead in providing for the poor. That was never meant to be the government's job, and it is no wonder these systems are corrupt.

Who is defending the rights of the needy? God asks the question, "Shall I not punish them for these things?" when referring to Israel and other nations. Sure, this was in light of a new, forthcoming covenant but do you really believe these issues of injustice did not come through the cross? Trust me, this does not change the responsibilities of the children of God. Who is Jesus talking about in Matthew 7 when He indicates that not everyone who calls on the name of the Lord will enter Heaven? Christ also warns that the gate to Heaven is small and the road is narrow.

These are sobering thoughts but is this truly not the cost of the blissful delusion of sitting on the sidelines believing we are running our race? Friends, this is a wake-up call for the Church. As believers, we must never allow a moment's distraction from the enemy. Instead, we need to be the disciples that Christ calls us to be. We need to have enough faith to start running in a life led by Him. We must strive for the "costly grace" that can only be found in obedience to Jesus. Anything less is simply catastrophic.

Be encouraged though; it isn't difficult to get started. It does, however, take humility before the Lord. One of the greatest examples I know of someone getting into their race is a friend of mine named Pete Ochs. Pete was a successful investment banker who, by all appearances, had everything. At forty years of age, he was financially independent and started his own firm. He had a strong marriage and two successful kids who were walking with the Lord. Even as a Christian, he appeared to be doing everything right. He was plugged into a healthy church which he regularly attended, and he even volunteered in the community.

Yet Pete sensed he hadn't started his race.

He says in his book, *A High Impact Life*[3],

> We had it all. Or so it seemed. So, why the dissatisfaction? With a troubled spirit, I began a process of inner reflection. I prayed, talked to friends, included my wife in examining every facet of my life, and spent time reading the usual

[3] Ochs, Pete. *A High Impact Life: Love your Purpose, Live with Passion, Leverage your Platform*. Enterprise Stewardship, February 1, 2019

> books on the subject. Slowly, the pieces began to
> fall into place. And the picture was disturbing.
> All my pursuits of success shared a common
> measuring stick, and that measuring stick was
> ME. My pursuit of success was nothing more than
> a desire to build a life that was all about me.

Taking some liberty to paraphrase his testimony, I would argue that despite all his busyness, Pete realized he was not quite in the race. I highly recommend making Pete's book part of your future reading but to sum it up, through prayer, counsel, and contemplation, he determined he would begin taking action to live a life wholly devoted to Christ. Pete decided to get in the race.

Now, Pete didn't sell off everything he had nor did he start wearing sackcloth. He didn't even run off to a cave in the desert to be quiet with God (although, I am confident he would have if he felt the Lord's leading). What he did do was clear the distractions and he took the time to *listen*. He sought the Lord regarding His "big picture" calling on Pete's life. Pete refers to a great quote from the Westminster Catechism, "Man's chief end is to glorify God and enjoy Him forever," so that's what he set out to do. As a result of this focused search, the Lord led him to recognize that he had the ability and proven success in identifying and building businesses. Pete dug for the root and found what he describes as his *ultimate purpose.*

Today Pete leads a successful financial firm dedicated to building businesses that glorify God. One of the businesses in his firm's portfolio is a seat company that makes a variety of products for agricultural and commercial uses. What makes this organization unique is that a majority of its staff and production live and work behind prison walls. Yes, Pete's company employs mostly prisoners.

Inmates are afforded the opportunity to earn a real wage while serving their time. Additionally, the company sponsors theological training to help the men grow in their faith at the same time. Pete's business behind prison walls provides a model for how industry can not only help rehabilitate inmates but change the stigma attached to the incarcerated. Not only are men taught new skillsets but their faith is deepened in both God and man. If Pete had not determined to get in the race, we might never have this paradigm of incorporating business and spiritual growth among the incarcerated. Pete teamed up with the organization I lead—Lifeline Global Ministries (LGM)—and we run our *Malachi Dads* program for the incarcerated at Hutchinson Correctional in Kansas where Pete runs his company.

If Pete could do it, so could you. But what is the secret?

Theologian Richard Rohr explains it in his book *The Gift of Contemplative Prayer*[4],

> Spirituality is about seeing. It's not about earning or achieving. It's about relationship rather than results or requirements. Once you see, the rest follows. You don't need to push the river, because you are in it. The life is lived within us, and we learn how to say yes to that life. If we exist on a level where we can see how "everything belongs," we can trust the flow and trust the life, the life so large and deep and spacious that it even includes its opposite, death.

Here is the secret: getting in the race means starting to refine our views. It means providing Christ the opportunity to flush the scales from our eyes so we can see the truth of our race. To be precise Rohr asks how we, as Christians, view the "least of these" (Matthew 25:40). Do we see Christ among the broken

---

[4] Rohr, Richard. *Everything Belongs: The Gift of Contemplative Prayer.* Crossroad, Revised and updated edition, March 1, 2003

of the world? More important, do we lift a hand to bring some measure of comfort to Him among the least of these?

As a man who has had the opportunity to serve in many third-world nations, I can tell you that these environments can be downright brutal. The dirt, the disease, the filth, and the odor are often overwhelming. And these characteristics are not relegated to only impoverished countries—walk among the slums of the United States and you witness many of the same things.

I have a friend who runs a ministry dedicated to the homeless in Los Angeles. His organization's area of operation has been known to house the largest population of homeless in America— the community affectionately named, "Skid Row." It can be near impossible for folks to walk into this community and see the face of Jesus. Many people, Christian and non-Christian, see this group of people as a nuisance. At best they might be on welfare and at worst they are a drain on our tax system. Yet Andy and his team are in the race, day in and day out. By getting into the race, they perceived things differently. They view life from a heavenly perspective.

In the same light, Rohr says[5],

> When we can see the image of God where we don't want to see the image of God, then we see with eyes not our own. The ability to respect the outsider is probably the litmus test of true seeing. It doesn't even stop with human beings and enemies and the least of the brothers and sisters. It moves to frogs and pansies and weeds. Everything becomes enchanting with true sight. One God, one world, one truth, one suffering, and one love. All we can do is participate.

[5] IBID

To participate, we must be *present* in the moment. *Now* is the time. Our biblical instruction is to not wait until the time is right but rather we are called to be in the race *now* in the manifestation of our minds and hearts through our faith in the saving grace of Christ. Today is the time; where you are is the place.

This does not necessarily imply that you need to sell your possessions and go serve with Andy and his team on Skid Row. What it means is that God has a very specific and tailor-made purpose for your life and you will *never* identify this call from the sidelines. You cannot put this off until the New Year. Who knows how much time each of us has to wait. . ? It has to be today. It must be now or it will likely be never.

I encourage you to be intentional with your time and make a decision to get in the race. Pastor Bill Hybels says in his book *Simplify*[6] that in order to make time for it, you need to add it to your calendar. In adding it to your calendar, you deliberately carve space out of the rat race to be in your *heavenly* race.

Faith Without Action is Dead

I once received an email from a church-planting pastor friend who had received a Tweet from John Piper. In the Tweet, Piper says, "What matters is that you keep your hand on the plow. You don't need to know what God will do through your work" (Ecclesiastes 8:17). How true this statement is. God wants us in the race because that is what He designed us for. To run joyfully with a heavenly vision. Furthermore, as Christians, we can be encouraged we have already made the team. It is clear that if we call on Jesus as our Lord and Savior and ask for forgiveness for our sins we are lovingly and mercifully accepted onto the "Heaven Team" due to Jesus' sacrifice at Calvary. But God wants more

---

[6] Hybels, Bill. *Simplify: Ten Practices to Unclutter Your Soul.* Tyndale Momentum; Paperback Reprint edition, May 1, 2015.

of us than just sitting on the bench. He is not satisfied with our hanging out with our letterman jackets letting everyone know we are on the team. God wants us in the game … He needs us in the race.

John Piper wisely states in his aptly titled book *Don't Waste Your Life*[7], "Life is wasted when we do not live for the glory of God." We cannot worry about whether we are good at it or if we still need a lot of practice. As Solomon said in Ecclesiastes 8:17, God just wants us to put our hand on the plow. Just get started. After reading this chapter I encourage you to take the time to determine if you are running the race in which God placed you. And are you actually racing or just believing you are, simply going through the motions on the sidelines?

Don't wait for the perfect morning. You don't need to go out and buy the right pair of running shoes. Don't worry if you are out of shape, out of practice, or even if you have never raced before. In this race, the Lord knows right where you are. He deeply desires for you to start running your race. He has plans for you that you can't even imagine right now. Things He wants to accomplish through you that you would hardly believe.

Now is the time. Get started.

[7] Piper, John. *Don't Waste Your Life*. Kindle Edition, Location 282-89. Crossway May 16, 2003.

TWO

Determine Your Starting Point

"It was becoming clearer and clearer that if I wanted to come to the end of my life and not say, "I've wasted it!" then I would need to press all the way in, and all the way up, to the ultimate purpose of God and join him in it. If my life was to have a single, all satisfying, unifying passion, it would have to be God's passion."[8]

John Piper

IMAGINE SITTING IN YOUR OFFICE ONE DAY WHEN SUDDENLY someone comes up behind you, restrains you, blindfolds you, binds your hands and feet, and loads you into a car. You can't see anything but you feel yourself being driven to what you can hear is a train station. After being put onto a train and traveling a few hours you arrive at an airport where you are transferred onto a plane. You experience vertigo as the plane lifts off and what feels like six hours later, you are bustled off the plane, placed back into a car, and driven for approximately three more hours. When the car stops, you are dropped off on a dirt road. You hear the vehicle drive away and work frantically to loosen the bindings on your

---

[8] Piper, John, *Don't Waste Your Life*, Kindle Edition, Location 237-43.

hands and feet. Able to free yourself you remove your blindfold and find yourself alone at a four-way intersection in the middle of nowhere. There are no road signs and the topography is such that you could be in any one of a dozen dry climates. In your back pocket, you find an envelope containing a note with the instruction: *Find Your Way Home.*

Believe it or not, this is the scenario many of us face when considering the future. We want to get in the race but find ourselves asking, "Where do I go from here?" A crucial bit of advice most life coaches, physical trainers, and medical professionals will give you is before you choose a direction, *find out where you are.*

How do you determine the starting point for your race? A more pressing question is *where do you need to be to join the race?*

Where Do You Need to Be?

An indication of where we need to be is found in Paul's letter to the Romans:

> Do not present your members to sin as instruments
> for unrighteousness, but present yourselves to
> God as those who have been brought from death
> to life, and your members to God as instruments
> for righteousness. Romans 6:13

Being "instruments for righteousness" means our lifestyle should attest to us being a member of the Church of Jesus Christ, and the temple of the Holy Spirit. In other words, everyone ought to recognize you as a Christian by the way you live and serve God in daily life. Psalm 50:5 says: "Gather to me faithful ones, who have made a covenant with me by sacrifice!" This is profound: notice what God uses as a definition of faithfulness—our covenant of sacrifice. This means it's not enough to simply call ourselves Christians, read our Bible and attend church once a week.

Jesus made this clear to the religious people of His day when He called them out saying, "Woe to you, scribes and Pharisees, hypocrites! For you clean the outside of the cup and the plate, but inside they are full of greed and self-indulgence" (Matthew 23:25). For more precise direction, Paul provides additional clarity further on in his letter to the Romans:

> ¹I appeal to you therefore, brothers, by the mercies of God, to present your bodies as a living sacrifice, holy and acceptable to God, which is your spiritual worship. ²Do not be conformed to this world, but be transformed by the renewal of your mind, that by testing you may discern what is the will of God, what is good and acceptable and perfect. Romans 12:1-2

So we see we are to offer ourselves as living sacrifices, but what does that mean? Do we offer ourselves fully as a living sacrifice to God in our daily walk? Do we start each day saying "Jesus, I don't know what You have in store for me but whatever it is—I accept!" We agree when we hear someone pray "Lord, not my will but Thy will," but do we apply the same principle to our lives?

Think of it this way: if we were placed in Jesus' parable of the Good Samaritan (Luke 10:29-37) would we be the priest, the Levite, or the Samaritan? It wasn't long ago that I would see a man on the side of the road asking for money and my worldly instincts would tempt me to think *Get a job*. This was *my will* talking—the will of my flesh. I have since taught myself to say, "Lord, you wouldn't put them in front of me if they didn't need my help," and when they ask I now give to them. This is submitting to *His will!* Whether they needed help or were ripping me off really doesn't matter. Doesn't the scripture say "And if anyone would sue you and take your tunic, let him have your cloak as well" (Matthew 5:40)?

History also has a way of showing us how to start a journey. Legend has it that when Spanish conquistador, Hernán Cortés, landed his boats in the new world to claim the country, he was so committed to making a success of it that he burned his boats (he actually sank them but the legend is close). Are you willing to burn your boats as an "all-in" sacrificial act of worship? Are you willing to "walk in a manner worthy of the calling to which you have been called" (Ephesians 4:1)?

Look at Where You Are

If you are still having difficulty in identifying where God wants you to start the race, look no further than where He already has you. God is very specific with our callings, so truly, your calling may begin with anything from being a laborer, an architect, teacher, or garbage collector. Finding your starting point does not necessarily mean you need to move towns or change jobs.

Too often, Christians, whether new or not, seem to think they need to be in just the right place to start their ministry. They want to orchestrate the perfect situation before they become engaged. Be honest with yourself and see if any of these statements apply to your mindset:

- I am really swamped, but as soon as my busyness recedes, I will look at starting my ministry.
- Right now, I am focused on career growth. As soon as I reach my goal, I will get engaged.
- Once I pay off my financial debts, I will have the freedom to do ministry.
- I am not in a place where ministry is an option.

To each of these, I would respond with "God has you where you are for a reason." Your launch point can be right where you find yourself. Embarking on a ministry adventure looks different for every person. Some of you may be called to start out as being the voice of peace and wisdom in a turbulent office. A launch point could be creating a healthy workplace in an industry known for taking advantage of low-paid workers. You may even have the opportunity to mentor younger colleagues, or perhaps evangelize coworkers who see the difference in the way you live and treat others. The point is if you are looking for a spot to start, you have an opportunity right where God has you now ... your vocation.

For many people, their calling is tied to their career. They may have never looked at it this way but this is generally how it is. Typically, we felt led to the industry in which we find ourselves, and to our role in the company. We trained for our work life through academic learning or apprenticeships and this is not by happenstance. Rather, we are given gifts and talents by God, and it is His supernatural power at work, orchestrating Kingdom life here on Earth that leads us into what we enjoy because we are called to a similar form of ministry.

A majority of our days are dedicated to our careers. Our relationships tend to be rooted in our workplaces so it again makes sense that this is the place the Lord has called many of us to. We may think we arrived in our career without the Lord's intervention, but He knows our every step before it is taken. He has opened and closed doors to lead us right where we are.

Our careers usually reflect an aspect of our calling, and our calling has been designed by God to help develop our spiritual growth. In his book *A Severe Mercy,* Sheldon Vanauken recalls C.S. Lewis' reply to his question of whether he should enter "Christian Ministry." C.S. Lewis' reply was, "The performance of duty will probably teach you quite as much about God as academic Theology would do."[9] This is a valuable insight, but

---

[9] Vanauken, Sheldon. 1987. *A Severe Mercy.* San Francisco: HarperCollins Publishers.

more importantly, our vocation is an opportunity for Jesus to live through us. Our lives in Christ are reflected in our day-to-day dealings in the workplace. In the same letter, Lewis goes on to say we certainly should, and must, bring God into our daily work. Our vocations rest with us whether we recognize them or not. It's not enough to sing songs of adoration on a Sunday and to pray daily devotions. These are good, but God makes clear His expectation of how we are to show Him reverence through our spiritual act of worship—by reflecting Him in everything we do, especially at work.

Living Here and Now—Dallas Willard

In the previous chapter, we learned that when Pete Ochs determined to get in the race, he spent time seeking counsel from others, and time in prayer and in contemplation listening for God's voice. This provides a terrific action framework for those who are tired of sitting on the sidelines considering their next move.

Too often, we find ourselves stuck in routines, bogged down by things of lesser importance. Our focus at times may lie solely on what is ahead, while at other times we find ourselves overly contemplating the past. I'm not saying considering the future or even past experiences are inconsequential because scripture makes it clear that thinking about the future is a sensible practice. Concerning the future, Psalm 90:12 says, "Teach us to number our days that we may get a heart of wisdom," and in the New Testament, Jesus asks the question, "For which of you, desiring to build a tower, does not first sit down and count the cost, whether he has enough to complete it?" (Luke 14:28). In the same vein, the book of Deuteronomy reflects on wisdom that may be gained from reviewing the past, "Remember the days of old; consider the years of many generations; ask your father, and he will show you, your elders, and they will tell you" (Deuteronomy 32:7). Paul adds his support to this in Romans 15:4 by saying: "For whatever was written in former days was written for our instruction."

Now to balance the wisdom of considering the past and the future, we should not get overly caught up in one or the other, losing sight of today. If we do we'll miss opportunities staring right at us in the present. Determining your starting point is difficult if you lack the ability to determine where you are "here and now." This holds true in all aspects of life, including our spiritual life and the ministry flowing from it.

Someone who had a handle on this, writing many foundational pieces on the subject, was Dallas Willard. Willard used his platform as an academic to generate discussion around living for Christ in the here and now. Written over the course of decades, his material and books, including *Renovation of the Heart*[10] and The *Divine Conspiracy*[11], are masterpieces in Christian literature.

Dr. Willard highlighted the fact that Christians frequently miss the opportunity to experience Christ in the present. He explains that too often we focus on the atonement and everlasting life, arguing that because of this we miss the opportunity to experience Heaven on Earth. In other words (my words), in focusing solely on what Christ did for us in His humanity (past actions), and what He offers us in eternal life (future actions), we risk missing the starting point (the present opportunity of daily relationship with Him).

This is what he says in his book *Divine Conspiracy*,

"He comes where we are, and he brings us the
life we hunger for. An early report reads, 'Life was
in him, life that made sense of human existence'

[10] Willard, Dallas. 2012. *Renovation of the Heart: Putting on the Character of Christ*. Colorado Springs, Colo.: Navpress.
[11] Willard, Dallas. 1998. *The Divine Conspiracy: Rediscovering Our Hidden Life in God*. San Francisco: Harper San Francisco.

(John 1: 4). To be the light of life, and to deliver God's life to women and men where they are and as they are, is the secret of the enduring relevance of Jesus. Suddenly they are flying right-side up, in a world that makes sense. Entering the Ordinary He slipped into our world through the backroads and outlying districts of one of the least important places on earth and has allowed his program for human history to unfold ever so slowly through the centuries. He lived for thirty years among socially insignificant members of a negligible nation—though one with a rich tradition of divine covenant."[12]

Entering the ordinary, as Willard explains it, is Christ's ability to meet us where we are … which is where we find our starting point!

What I appreciate about Dr. Willard was the example he set in living out what he preached. I had the blessed opportunity to speak with him briefly during my doctoral program at Pepperdine University. I was doing a study on leadership at the highest levels of success and not only was I trying to identify leaders who would provide great examples for my study, but also those who would actually give me the time to interview them.

At the time, Dallas was a faculty member at USC despite his advanced years, and any time with him was much sought after. I honestly didn't think I had a shot at getting to interview him but left a message with a request anyway. The research team I was a part of was having difficulty getting access to top-level leaders such as various corporate CEOs and the head of the Navy Seals; we were struggling to either connect with them or find an adequate time to schedule interviews. Imagine my

[12] Ibid

surprise when an unrecognized number on my cell phone turned out to be Dallas Willard returning my call. I could not believe that in between writing books, teaching sessions, doing lectures, conferences, and other engagements, he took the time to return my call and talk to me.

I would love to tell you that we spoke for hours; that we became the best of buddies, and that he invited me over for dinner to further discuss my project, but that didn't happen. My call with him was brief but wonderful, leaving an extremely positive impact on my life. Dallas not only found the starting point in his life, but he also wanted to ensure other Christian leaders found theirs as well. Finding your starting point is not as intimidating as it may seem.

Easier than You Think

Earlier we discussed the busyness of work-life and a career, and coupled with busy family life, the thought of starting a ministry may simply appear too daunting. I want to make it clear that finding your starting point and getting into the race does not have to mean starting your own ministry. There are many existing ministries where you can be faithful to your covenant of sacrifice by offering your time and experience. In fact, many people are called to what is known as the Ministry of Helps— assisting the Five-fold Ministry (Apostle, Prophet, Evangelist, Pastor, and Teacher).

There are many avenues of ministry, so be open to where the Holy Spirit may lead you. Lifeline Global (LGM) is where God led me and this ministry has been a complete Godsend for my life. It is also a good example of how to get into the race using programs and tools already in existence. If you *still* have no idea where to start, I don't know … maybe you're reading this book for a reason. LGM has many materials for anyone wanting to get in the race and make an impact in their community; you could start by serving in one of ours. Children desperately need their fathers and mothers to lead and direct them and the *Malachi Dads* and *Hannah's Gift* programs work to restore and equip incarcerated men and women so they can become godly parents and break the generational cycle of incarceration. If you're really stumped, pray about which of LGM's existing ministries God wants you to become involved with, and how to arrange your time to be an instrument for righteousness.

Also, through our sacrifice to Him—our conforming to His example—the Lord reveals to us His plans for our life. We gain a clearer sense of who we are called to be, and what we are called to do. Paul tells us that where you focus your mind is where you will find yourself (Romans 8:5-8). This is why Paul urges you instead, to be transformed by the renewal of your mind that by testing you may discern what is the will of God (Romans 12:2). Renewing your mind with the Word of God allows you wisdom and discernment to follow the paths that Christ has laid out for you. I want to encourage you to honestly consider how you respond to God's holiness and mercy; have you offered yourself as a living sacrifice? Have you burned your boats?

Once we have performed this self-evaluation—this litmus test if you will—we gain a clearer picture of what sort of racing shape we are in. Some will find they are in better shape than they thought they were, others maybe not so much. Don't be discouraged, because we get to participate in the race regardless of our spiritual fitness levels. Start where you are. Being honest with yourself in this test allows the Lord to provide the instruction and guidance to find your starting point as well as the pace at which you should run. This determines how you are going to run the race from this point forward.

I've said there are many reasons to be distracted from finding your starting point. The author of Hebrews was aware that contestants stripped down to a loincloth for the race as clothes would hinder the athlete. He advises us to do the same in our spiritual walk, saying, "Let us also lay aside every weight and sin which clings so closely, and let us run with endurance the race that is set before us" (Hebrews 12:1). Stripping down to the essentials is an analogy, not only about removing sin from your life but removing all the other hindrances and distractions too.

Don't sit on the sidelines in the delusion of being a spectator. Get in the race as the contestant you were called to be!

Once you have found your starting point and you set off from the line, excited to be in the race, you will find the support and direction of experienced runners who are invaluable to your race.

Stick with me because in the next chapter we will cover who and what is needed for you to run a good race.

THREE

Find Good Coaches

Without counsel plans fail,
but with many advisers they succeed.
Proverbs 15:22

AMY AND I RECENTLY HAD A FRIEND OVER TO VISIT WHOSE SPOUSE is a top-ranking amateur triathlete. This in itself is impressive, but what amazes me about Julie is she is also a full-time homemaker and mom to two very active kids. When I pressed my friend, Steve, about how his wife managed to keep up the pace she does he listed several traits of hers that I already suspected she possessed. Steve told me she is focused, competitive, manages time well, and trains hard. Being a triathlete is an individual activity and not a team sport, so there was another strength of hers that caught me by surprise: what I hadn't expected was the group of people with which she surrounds herself. While *professional* athletes typically have an entourage surrounding them, the number of people Julie has around her to make all of this happen was a revelation.

Julie has swimming coaches to analyze her swimming technique and help with her stroke, running coaches and training partners to push her to the next level, and a variety of other partners and coaches who assist her in achieving this high level of competition. Steve also explained that over time she has made changes to her training style and even her coaches. Just as she has worked hard to perfect the disciplines of running, biking, and swimming, Julie has exercised the same diligence in sourcing excellent coaches.

What Steve didn't say, however, is that he is the consistent coach she has maintained over time. At the beginning of each season, she and Steve sit down and map out what the coming season will look like. This includes which events she will participate in, and how the training for each event will be approached. Although Steve is not a triathlete, his forte is providing good direction on which goals to shoot for, and assistance in plotting the path to achieve those objectives.

After speaking with Steve about the way in which Julie approaches her sport, I immediately saw the similarities required in the spiritual race all Christians are running. Proverbs 24:6 tells us, "For by wise guidance you will wage war, And in abundance of counselors there is victory." One of the keys to living an effective Christian life is to surround yourself with good counsel. Jesus made it clear that we are to go out and make disciples (Matthew 28:19), but how many of us remember that we are also called to *be* disciples? As Christians, our spiritual development is ongoing, and though God has provided us with different gifts and skillsets, this does not mean we are all blessed with the same amount of discernment. In His Word, God advises us to surround ourselves with mentors, coaches, and friends. These people are there to offer advice and guidance, providing the wisdom and the accountability we need for our continued growth.

Sports coaches have the ability to overhaul the dynamics of movement to help you excel in your sport, and often provide the nagging voice telling you to keep pushing no matter how much you want to give up. Good coaches are right there with words of encouragement no matter what obstacles you may be facing. They know your potential. Godly coaches are those who focus not on whether you win or lose, but rather on how much effort you apply to seek the Lord. They are the ones who are as willing to put their arm around you during the depths of failure as they are to hug you in the exhilaration of victory.

For those who feel they can make it on their own, Jesus cautions us on the road ahead: "For the gate is narrow and the way is hard that leads to life, and those who find it are few" (Matthew 7:14). The road of our spiritual race ahead is not an easy one, and we are going to need help and assistance. We are not designed to go it alone; the Lord created us for communion and planned for us to seek counsel, find that trusted mentor, and have accountability partners. As Christ indicates, it is not a wide-open finish line that awaits us—the gate is narrow and few find it.

We can debate what He means by the word "few," but if Christ meant to use the word "many" He would have. The implication of this statement is that we are competing at a very high level. To be one of the few who find the narrow gate on the hard way leading to life, we will need direction and assistance in our spiritual walk. Good coaches help us understand direction and teach us what is needed to stay on the path. Godly coaches help to fine-tune our daily walk so the way to life does not seem so hard. They will ensure we live in tiptop spiritual shape to compete at the high standard required of us. There is not an elite athlete out there who does not have a coach or two. If you are in the same race I am, I strongly suggest you find yourself some good coaches as well.

In all aspects of life, being successful takes hard work, dedication, commitment, and perseverance. Ultimately, though, there is only so far we can go on our own. Once we have reached the pinnacle of our solo efforts, it is crucial we identify a good coach who can help us achieve our goals. The right coach provides an insightful game plan because they see and understand the landscape a little differently than we might. If collaboration and cooperation are required, coaches can assist in strengthening teamwork. They understand the intricacies that go into preparatory training, are generally aware of the potential pitfalls we may face, and possess the knowledge to navigate these issues when they arise. Most importantly, a good coach can see the light at the end of the tunnel, and whether through experience or wisdom, the coach understands what it will take to reach the success you are aiming for.

Our lives in ministry are no different from an athlete participating in a high-level event. With God's grace, accompanied by our own efforts, we learn to live The Great Commission. This implies that we should be open with our faith and look to build discipling relationships. For some, this practice of building discipling relationships pulls them well outside their comfort zone. For others, the practice of carrying out The Great Commission propels them into the next phase of their life in Christ. This could be a more profound walk of faith into some of the other examples of ministry that Christ and the early Church walked in. It also means allowing some of Christ's deeper teaching like those we find in Matthew 25 to sink deeply into our hearts. The teachings in Matthew 25 show how we are to be willfully ready in the service of the Lord, and those who aren't, risk severe consequences. This is shown in the parable of the ten virgins, the parable of the bag of gold, and the account of the sheep and the goats.

Walking in these examples of ministry and the teaching of Matthew 25 means we need to be fully *in the race*. On one hand, we need mentors and coaches to assist us in our spiritual walk, and on the other, we need to *be* the mentors and coaches discipling other people. In fact, in many instances, we need coaching on how to disciple others. This is where I find ministries like LGM to be so valuable. What makes the LGM curriculum such a powerful tool is that our material provides everything needed for both the mentor and the disciple.

I also believe LGM is especially suited to this critical discipling-centric ministry. We frequently hear of people reluctant to engage in ministry to the incarcerated because they are nervous about teaching people from a potentially different walk of life. Too often, people feel they do not have enough biblical knowledge to adequately train other men or women. Some even think they need a Master of Divinity degree or a Theology doctorate to have an impact in our classes. Nothing could be farther from the truth.

The reason LGM's curriculum is so effective is that it was designed from a coach's perspective. We make it easy to engage with incarcerated students in that our material entails *facilitating* rather than teaching. Both the Malachi Dads and Hannah's Gift programs are laid out so the person leading the discussion can simply open to page one and begin reading from the script. Throughout the text and training, there are prompts to the facilitator as to where the conversation should be taken next. The training utilizes a group dynamic and encourages all students to participate and be involved.

For those needing more instruction, we have a How-To guide available on our website, which is a verbal coaching tutorial developed to assist the facilitator. For facilitators who would like further training, we have a separate curriculum called Equip Leaders which provides an in-depth overview of all facilitation. And finally, for anyone who prefers hands-on training, this can be accomplished in person or over a Zoom video call.

I think LGM becomes more than just a ministry for the incarcerated because our success is rooted in being good coaches for *all* the people we work with. I believe this happened naturally due to the unique nature of training people to minister to the incarcerated. Our coaching method has become such a powerful discipling method because we have to carefully train (or disciple) those who will be discipling the incarcerated. The bottom line is to not only minister to the incarcerated, but to provide the means for *you* to get in the race, and to ensure you are adequately equipped for the success of your ministry!

The Impact of Good Coaching

The reason I am so passionate about coaching and mentorship is that I have experienced the benefits of guidance and coaching in my own life and ministry. When I analyzed the course of my life, one thing became abundantly clear—I have had great coaches. I would love to say there is a secret sauce to any of the success I have enjoyed, or that I was born with all kinds of talent. I might even be tempted to say that God decided to ordain me for accomplishment at an early age, but the truth of the matter is that any success I have enjoyed is due primarily to the work of others in my life. God has blessed me with great mentors—or coaches if you will. Better yet, I define a good coach as a Disciple Maker.

From childhood to manhood I am eternally grateful to have had both my parents actively involved in my life. My dad taught me the importance of a firm handshake and the commitment to stand behind it. I learned the value of a hard day's work and had a constant picture of the responsibility it takes to be the head of the household. The role my dad played while I was growing up and the impact he has had on my life is one of the reasons I was so drawn to working with LGM. For many, living in the world can be difficult enough. Many people have not had the benefit of godly parents I had. LGM helps to fill the void of the lack of godly parenting for many children.

As an adult I have experienced the great privilege of having men walk with me, guide me, and encourage me at crucial times in my life. I will not list the many who have coached me over the years but will say that these coaches influenced almost every aspect of my life. Their influence spans my time in the military as well as my professional career. I also had the added benefit of godly men who helped coach me on how to be a better dad and husband.

Finding good coaches admittedly takes some work, though. Of key importance is finding someone with shared interests.

Coaches I gravitated towards were typically men who had already achieved a certain amount of success in the areas in which I was engaged. Typically, these men had the character I wanted to emulate and were the type of leaders I desired to be. I also, however, looked for someone with the heart of a teacher. Proverbs 20:5 tells us, "The purpose in a man's heart is like deep water, but a man of understanding will draw it out." It is a special person who gains value by investing their time, knowledge, and experience in someone else. Once you find them, though, the learning lessons are endless.

Just like a good athletic coach, life coaches and those who disciple you in ministry are going to know when to push you, but will also be aware when you are pushing too hard. They tell you what you need to hear when you need to hear it. In my race, I required ministry mentors to sometimes kick me in the seat of the pants, while at other times I needed an arm of comfort around my shoulders.

As with other areas of my life, God has introduced me to a variety of individuals who would be instrumental in helping to shape my ministry life. I found my coach working with the incarcerated at what seemed like a chance meeting. At the time, I was working with a missions organization that worked in underserved communities around the nation. Mike Broyles had been a pastor at a large church in Southern California. Both of our ministries were transitioning when I was introduced to Mike whose calling was to build up godly parenting among the incarcerated. From that initial meeting, I was invited to see ministry being carried out at the Los Angeles County Jail where an entirely new world of ministry was opened up to me.

Mike is the Executive Director of LGM and one of the original architects who helped take the ministry from an idea at one prison and turn it into something tangible and replicable. Mike and I began working together over a decade ago and he continues to be a mentor in my life today. I still learn humility and grace from Mike's example. With his fifty-plus years of pastoring, I am challenged by both his level of activity and endurance. Mike is more than my colleague; he is also my coach.

At the beginning of this chapter, I mentioned that one of the characteristics Julie—my friend Steve's wife–has, is that she trains hard to achieve the goals she has set herself. Like all dedicated athletes, Julie trains to get her body into the shape required to compete at the high level she does. In a similar fashion, to attain the high standard required for the race we are running, it is vital we are in good spiritual and emotional shape. In the next chapter, we will discuss how we can go about getting into shape while we are in the race.

FOUR

Get in Shape along the Way

CAN I BE VERY REAL WITH YOU? I *REALLY* DO NOT ENJOY WORKING out. Yeah, I said it. Working out is often the last thing in the world I want to do. Don't get me wrong … after I finish a workout I feel great and I am so happy I did it but leading into the workout, I am a total bear. Seriously, sometimes I turn into a two-year-old. I may not kick and scream, but I pout and glare; especially if it is an early morning workout. My wife, on the other hand, loves to get up at the crack of dawn for some bright, ultra-enthusiastic exercise. She practically springs out of bed and sings about how wonderful it is to be alive. I wake up in the morning frustrated that the Lord did not take me in my sleep (my wife tells me this is extremely morbid).

I am simply not cut from the same cloth as my wife. The standing rule is there is to be no talking until we get to the track, which is about a mile and a half away. It just takes me time to wake up and kick-start my "happy engine." Maybe it was all those years in the military that made me this way. I just have a hard time wrapping my brain around getting up so early unless I am forced to.

Once the exercise begins, I hate to admit I am no better. I work my way around the track counting down how many meters

I have left until it is over. I really *want* to be one of those people who get out there because they love it because it is with these people I share the track. But I am simply not one of these people, and if I was going to change I believe it would have happened by now. I am a big guy who has been blessed with a wife who is a great cook. I long for the day I can eat whatever I want to but unfortunately, I am the type who exercises frequently and can still put on weight. The reason I work out is that *I have to.*

I'll be the first to point out that my perspective on exercise is not a good one. It is an attitude on which I have worked, and I will continue to do so. But it still takes work. The one thing I *do* love about exercising is that I get to spend quality time with the Lord, and some quality time with my wife. My entire drive to the track is spent in communion with my heavenly Father as I prepare my mind and heart for the day ahead. It is during this time I begin to recognize and appreciate what a joy it is to spend time with my wife as we get to bring in the day together at the track. I also realize it is a privilege I am healthy enough to push my body, if not for myself then for the Lord so I can better serve Him. Most importantly, it is a gift to have time in which I can confer with my Father about His will for my life.

I am reminded of what Paul tells us in Romans 5:3-4 when he tells us that we are to rejoice in all things. He goes on to say, "³ Not only that, but we rejoice in our sufferings, knowing that suffering produces endurance, ⁴ and endurance produces character, and character produces hope." I am ashamed at how quickly I forget this, yet it is natural in our humanness that we only consider ourselves in our struggles. All our lives we have been programmed to relieve pain and suffering as quickly as we can. Modern medicines have been designed to do just that; in fact, the basis of the addictions that plague our world are a result of people wanting to drown out their pain.

Of course, I would never equate my time on the track to the real suffering that takes place in the world each and every day. I just need to flip on the TV and the realities of the vast pain on this planet become quickly apparent. Rather, I am wondering what would happen if we changed our perspective on suffering? What if we took Paul's advice and rejoiced in suffering instead of trying to snuff it out as quickly as possible? Mind you, I am not advocating the need for forced suffering or asceticism. We should never create our own suffering so we can have something to rejoice in. We should rather embrace the call of God on our lives, recognizing that suffering is sometimes part of His will. Indeed, the apostle Peter tells us:

> [19] For this is a gracious thing, when, mindful of God, one endures sorrows while suffering unjustly. [20] For what credit is it if, when you sin and are beaten for it, you endure? But if when you do good and suffer for it you endure, this is a gracious thing in the sight of God. 1 Peter 2:19-20

But where does that leave us? Are we to go out and look for righteous suffering? Is that even possible? I don't believe we should go out and search for suffering; on the contrary, enough can be found to wholeheartedly embrace right under our noses.

Personally, I can do a better job of embracing the opportunity at hand when I exercise. Although I may never fully enjoy the exercise, I can still rejoice in the chance to draw closer to God and remain healthy to effectively lead my family. I can take also solace that my daily grind is forging a better me. Not the physical part of me *per se,* but more so the spiritual component. Just as Paul said, my struggles enhance my perseverance which in turn helps build my character.

I also don't have to be perfect. Although I may not enjoy exercising today, who knows what can happen in the future? I may come to love it. This is why I don't try to have a perfect attitude when I wake up—that would be insincere. No, I'm becoming perfect along the way as the apostle Paul said in Philippians 3:12, "Not that I have already obtained this or am already perfect, but I press on to make it my own, because Christ Jesus has made me his own."

We must remember that we don't wake up in shape—we get in shape along the way. This relieves the pressure but there is still an element of pressing on, as Paul said. How do we press on? We embrace with joy the little bits of suffering we face each day. We do our best to better ourselves daily, and truly it should come out of love for those around us. We strive in the small challenges even in the face of seemingly persistent setbacks, because we never know the full story. Something life-changing may be just around the corner.

An account related on LGM's website is a good illustration of someone trying to stay in shape as a dad to his two daughters while forced to be physically absent from their lives. Darwin "Hutch" Hutchinson had been in Angola prison for seventeen years, being incarcerated when his two daughters were seven and eight years old. After seven years in prison, Hutchinson experienced his first Returning Hearts Celebration; his daughters were then fourteen and fifteen. This event encouraged Hutch and his children to treasure their relationship as father and daughters but the relationship-building process was not always an easy one. Hutchinson was allowed to send cards to his daughters to maintain communication, but for every dozen cards he sent he would get maybe one response back. It was a bit discouraging, to say the least, but he was determined to stay firm because he knew, as a Malachi Dad, how crucial it was to pursue the relationship, no matter the struggle and perseverance required.

When his youngest daughter turned twenty-one Hutchinson had sent a card for her birthday, but she was also old enough to freely communicate with her dad over the phone instead of through just cards and letters. He called to ask if she received it and she told him yes, she had, but she had a dilemma: she had no more room on her wall. Hutchinson didn't understand. He believed only a few of his cards had made it through to her. He couldn't have been more wrong.

Not only had his daughter received all her cards over the years but she had also been putting her favorites up on her wall, and on her twenty-first birthday she had run out of room! She still had boxes of cards under her bed. Hutchinson's face broke into a wide smile and joy erupted in his heart when he found out his daughter had not only received his cards but she had treasured them so. Hutchinson's endurance had paid off. He wasn't perfect, but he had just glimpsed a touch of perfection in his relationship with his daughter.

"All along I was sending these cards, I was writing these letters, and I was doing so with the sole purpose of trying to build the bridge of communication when all along I was building a wall of cards," Hutchinson said. "Most people think of a wall as a barrier. This was more like a wall of fame." Hutchinson's daughters have since aged out of the program, being tremendously impacted by the program. As a result, Hutchinson is now able to spend time with his grandson.

When I heard of Hutchinson's persistence through his sufferings, striving for excellence even when the efforts seem pointless it reminded me of something I had read regarding Vice President (at the time) Theodore Roosevelt addressing a group of Yale and Harvard undergraduates:

> Roosevelt took the project with a good deal of seriousness going through some soul-searching to find out how to best help these young men recognize the importance of doing the little, humdrum elementary jobs of good citizenship in order to condition themselves to grasp the larger opportunities for service when later they came their way. That was how he himself had accomplished

> what he had. Not by genius, he had no particle
> of genius he was convinced, or even any unusual
> talent; he had merely done the commonplace, not
> very difficult things which in theory most men
> agreed should be done by everyone: the point
> was, you didn't need exceptional gifts to render
> notable, even exceptional service; anyone with a
> fair amount of common sense, courage, integrity,
> and physical hardihood could render it.[13]

I love how Roosevelt emphasized to young men the importance of cultivating *habits* over so-called genius. In my own striving to get in shape along the way, after graduating from college, one book I found extremely helpful was Stephen Covey's *The Seven Habits of Highly Successful People*. While I enjoyed a somewhat successful academic life, I wanted to absorb all I could from this book, especially as I established my professional career. To this day I find this book a useful read. It provided valuable advice on matters like being proactive, seeking to understand before being understood, and beginning with the end in mind.

In his book, Covey claimed that one could only play six to seven roles effectively at any one time, so at the end of every year, I would set time aside to go over my goal planning and tie it to each of these roles. I guess you could say I had made a habit of embracing the Seven Habits. It was embracing the so-called suffering of setting time aside, painstakingly mapping out each habit to a role, and contemplating my capacity and how each habit affected each role, that helped significantly expand my faith walk. As a direct result of doing something deliberate and stretching myself, I adopted increasingly positive habits each year.

Each year I would focus on goals for the six to seven roles I

---

[13] Hagedorn, Hermann. 1954. *The Roosevelt Family of Sagamore Hill*. New York, Macmillan.

played: Manager, Husband, Scout Leader, Father, etc. For years one of the roles would be "Christian." I would compartmentalize my role as a Christian and set a series of goals I thought the Lord wanted me to achieve that year. As time went on, however, I realized through prayer that the Lord did not at all desire for "Christian" to be one of my roles. He made it very clear that my faith walk was not one in a list of roles for which to set goals. Rather, my faith was to encompass every role I played and every part of my life. How my life changed from that realization.

Since that time, I still have a habit of penciling out habits and disciplines which I would like to adopt as part of my life. Now, though, in each of these, I look for Christ. This is the one habit that I would suggest we all have. In every activity you do, make sure you are looking for Christ. I know it sounds easy, but it really isn't. There are so many times we get caught up in ministry for ministry's sake and lose sight of our Savior. *Recognize the suffering therein, and embrace it.*

Forging habits and disciplines are a great way to move forward and get in shape along the way. Habit number one should always be to look for Christ. This is because the key to endurance lies in trusting God: "Those who trust in the Lord are like Mount Zion, which cannot be moved, but abides forever" (Psalm 125:1). This is not based on wishful thinking but on the character and protection of the God in whom we trust. Anything else in which we put our trust is ultimately futile because "Unless the Lord builds the house, those who build it labor in vain" (Psalm 127:1a). So let's keep building and see why you need to *pace yourself.*

FIVE

Pace Yourself

¹ The plans of the heart belong to man,
but the answer of the tongue is from the LORD.
² All the ways of a man are pure in his own eyes,
but the LORD weighs the spirit.
³ Commit your work to the LORD,
and your plans will be established.
Proverbs 16: 1-3

WOULD YOU AGREE THE LORD DESIRES US TO BE IN LINE WITH HIS calling on our lives? It is true that while He doesn't require us to constantly run at a pace we are not comfortable with, we are to stretch our capabilities. Once you have determined your starting point, you are in the race, you have sourced good coaches, and you begin to get into shape "that you may proclaim the excellencies of him who called you out of darkness into his marvelous light" (1 Peter 2:9). Then you will run at a pace to ensure you finish strong.

The key to finishing your race strong is to run at a pace you can maintain, relying on "him who called you" for endurance. Just as a good coach cautions a high-level athlete for pushing too hard in his or her efforts, we need to realize that racing headlong into ministry does not ensure success. Scripture supports this. In Ecclesiastes 9:11 we read, "Again I saw that under the sun the race is not to the swift ..." Burning yourself out before the finish line doesn't benefit you or your ministry, and certainly doesn't benefit the people to whom you are ministering. Likewise, however, plodding along with minimum advancement won't adequately fulfill the calling on your life. Balance is crucial. To this end, keep in mind that an important aspect of race motivation and endurance is an awareness of *why* you are running.

This concept was highlighted for me years back when a good friend of mine decided he was going to run the Chicago Marathon cold turkey. He was always in good shape but had not trained a lick for a race at that level. Having recently returned from serving a tour with the Peace Corps in Bolivia, and living in the mountains for the previous two years, he felt he could handle a race so close to sea level. I thought he was nuts, of course, and there was no way I was going to join him in this "adventure." I had no illusions of winning the race, but I know the adage "to finish first you must first finish,"[14] and I knew I was not in the condition required to even finish in a race of this magnitude. I was, however, happy to accompany him to the starting line and root him on through the race.

Now, if you have never been to a race of this scale you would be astonished at the fanfare surrounding it. It is a *colossal* event! Music blares across a huge throng of excited people, the *whomp whomp whomp* of helicopters can be deafening as they circle overhead, streets are closed off, and police cars and ambulances accompany the runners along the route. Just being in the crowd and watching the runners line up for the starting gun made my hair stand on end with anticipation. All the news agencies were there, and every one of them had their cameras glued to the starting line.

When the starting gun blasted, a handful of people took off at a full sprint. They ran like they were participating in a

---

[14] "Rick Mears Quotes." n.d. BrainyQuote. Accessed July 28, 2022. https://www.brainyquote.com/quotes/rick_mears_307678.

hundred-meter-dash, not a race that is over twenty-six miles long. Having run a few long-distance races myself, it amused me to see them take off that fast compared to the rest of the group. I was not surprised to see that less than a quarter mile later this same group exited the race. It suddenly became clear to me what they were doing. They were not interested in completing the race; they just wanted to be the runners leading the race out of the gate. This handful of early sprinters likely sought the temporary glory they enjoyed as the television crews captured them leading the pack at this grand event.

Even though it seems ludicrous to think people would go to this extent to see themselves on television, this isn't far off from how many of us approach the spiritual race in which God has placed us. At times we may be guilty of getting in the race purely for selfish motives, not being interested in how we run, or even finishing. We often feel it is more important to be *seen* as running the race.

If by this logic, it is so important to be seen to be in the race then it follows that our desire is to impress those watching. Very few, however, are impressed by someone leaving the race early, whether they began the race at a sprint for personal glory, or just didn't pace themselves to make it to the finish line. Hebrews 12:1-2 gives us an idea of why we are in the race we are, who is watching our race, and how to pace ourselves to make it to the finish line:

> [1] Therefore, since we are surrounded by so great a cloud of witnesses, let us also lay aside every weight, and sin which clings so closely, and let us run with endurance the race that is set before us, [2] looking to Jesus, the founder and perfecter of our faith, who for the joy that was set before him endured the cross, despising the shame, and is seated at the right hand of the throne of God. Hebrews 12:1-2

This is a powerful passage. When we break this verse down, much about our race becomes clear. The author of Hebrews begins chapter twelve with the word "Therefore," indicating what he is about to say follows from what he has previously said. In the previous chapter he listed many of the "Heroes of Faith," from Abel to Noah, then Abraham and Sarah, to Moses and David, naming some of the Judges, and mentioning the prophets. He then concludes with "³⁹ And all these, though commended through their faith, did not receive what was promised, ⁴⁰ since God had provided something better for us, that apart from us they should not be made perfect" (Hebrews 11:39-40). What the writer is saying is these heroes of faith never saw God's promise fulfilled, but now we have the fulfilment of that promise in Jesus and the Holy Spirit abiding on Earth.

The people of faith listed in Hebrews 11 is the great cloud of witnesses the author is referring to. They are eagerly watching how we make the most of the fulfilment that was promised from the beginning. If we are to run a successful race with this great cloud of witnesses surrounding us, we need to lay aside every weight that hampers our progress. The words *"every* weight" point to there being more than one type of weight that needs to be laid aside. These weights could include cares, worries, guilt, or a multitude of other burdens. In his letter to the Philippians, Paul explains how to deal with anxiety and cares that weigh us down:

> ⁶ do not be anxious about anything, but in everything by prayer and supplication with thanksgiving let your requests be made known to God. ⁷ And the peace of God, which surpasses all understanding, will guard your hearts and your minds in Christ Jesus. Philippians 4:6-7

Notice the conjunction "and" telling us that in order to run a successful race, laying aside every weight is not enough; we need to lay aside every *sin* too. We are told that these sins cling to us closely so it will take more than a conscious effort to rid ourselves of them. Part of God's fulfilled promise is the indwelling of the Holy Spirit Who was sent to help you overcome sin, and renew your mind *if* you are willing to surrender to Him. This is confirmed in Galatians 5:16 which tells us, "But I say, walk by the Spirit, and you will not gratify the desires of the flesh."

The second part of Hebrews 12:1 reminds us of the reason we are to lay aside every weight and sin: " …and let us run with endurance the race that is set before us …" By saying "let us" the author of Hebrews is reminding us that we have an option in the decision and have *chosen* to be in the race. More than that, God has provided us the *opportunity* to be in the race and to fulfill the calling on our lives. Furthermore, the phrase " …let us run …" means we can choose to walk but the directive is to run and to run with endurance. The most assured way of running with endurance is to pace yourself correctly. Sadly, the reason most cited by pastors considering leaving the ministry in 2021-2022 was pastoral burnout.[15] God's plan was never for you to become disillusioned with ministry, or to neglect your family and your health.

The words "we" and "us" in Hebrews 12:1 makes it clear we are not alone in the race. There are those running alongside us in ministry who we can support and from whom we can receive support. This is how you run with endurance. We are not meant to run on our own, because that adds an element of chronic fatigue. There is great strength in community. As I've mentioned, there are also mentors and coaches we can turn to when we feel our pace lagging or our endurance waning.

---

[15] "Pastors Share Top Reasons They've Considered Quitting Ministry in the Past Year." n.d. Barna Group. https://www.barna.com/research/pastors-quitting-ministry/.

By saying we should run with endurance, the author of Hebrews is telling us that the race set before us is a long race and we are therefore to run with sound methods (community) and at a pace in keeping with making it to the finish line. Always bearing in mind *Who* set the race before us will keep the race in perspective. We may have chosen to get in the race but the nature of the race is not one we choose—our race was set before us. There are many types of races and many people running, but we must pace ourselves for the specific and unique race set before us.

Furthermore, we are not called to be spectators at the race nor are we to be participants with no regard for how we run, or how long we run. God can't use you as He intended if you are not committed to finishing the race. Find the starting point, get in the race, and then pace yourself to the finish. There are many ministries geared to support you throughout your race; ministries like LGM who offer various starting points in ministry with the scope, opportunity, and support to move forward and grow at a pace that will ensure you finish strong. LGM's ultimate mission is generational restoration, but to achieve this requires community restoration, which begins with family restoration.

Becoming a part of the end goal of generational restoration may seem like a distant finish line, but it can start by volunteering for just one day at the Returning Hearts Celebration Event. At this event, the joy of seeing families being reunited has encouraged many to continue assisting in other areas, and even to become facilitators in the Malachi Dads or Hannah's Gift programs. In these well-structured programs, all the support required for a successful ministry to the incarcerated is provided. Surrounding yourself with this kind of guidance and support, your ministry will flourish at a pace matching your spiritual growth.

As discussed in Chapter Three, we are in a high-level race requiring us to be athletes of a high caliber. Elite athletes prepare and plan the course of their race. The enemy will try to hinder your advancement wherever he can so you need to recognize and be prepared to overcome the obstacles. In 2 Timothy 4:7, Paul, who was nearing the end of his life, said, "⁷I have fought the good fight, I have finished the race, I have kept the faith." No one calls a fight where they threw in the towel a "good fight." We know Paul faced many obstacles in his ministry by his letter to Timothy saying, "Three times I was beaten with rods. Once I was stoned. Three times I was shipwrecked; a night and a day I was adrift at sea" (2 Corinthians 11:25), yet he finished the race. Paul kept going by pacing himself to the finish line knowing the Lord stood by him and strengthened him, even when others abandoned him (2 Timothy 4:17).

God has an evangelistic plan for each one of us whether we know it or not, so we need to be aware of the danger of becoming so saturated in the church environment to the point where we rarely come into contact with non-Christians. We must never lose sight of the fact that we are called to be disciples and to make disciples of others within our sphere of influence. See your workplace as a place of ministry, where you can affect people in a positive way and share the love of God through your actions. We are called to not just preach the Word of God, but to *live* it; not to just go to church but to *be* the Church. Pacing yourself means being in touch with God at all times. We can't hear God if life consumes every moment of our day. We need to find a routine time to be quiet to be able to hear God or our race will lose direction. This quote on the subject resonates with me:

> Try to keep your soul always in peace and quiet, always ready for whatever our Lord may wish to work in you. It is certainly a higher virtue of the soul, and a greater grace, to be able to enjoy the Lord in different times and different places than in only one. —Ignatius of Loyola[16]

---

[16] "A Quote by Ignatius of Loyola." n.d. www.goodreads.com. Accessed July 29, 2022. https://www.goodreads.com/quotes/7337550-try-to-keep-your-soul-always-in-peace-and-quiet.

Pacing ourselves means we need to recognize and keep in mind that regardless of the pace we run, God is with us through it all just as He was with Paul. He stands by us and strengthens us. That being said, sometimes having someone run with you increases your motivation and encourages you to "get up and do it." You may even be the person who motivates *them* to get in the race by your example. In the next chapter, we will discuss why you should encourage others to join you in fighting the good fight and the immense benefits it can have on your life and ministry.

SIX

Encourage Others to Join You

HAVE YOU EVER SEEN THE YOUTUBE VIDEO WHERE A GUY IS AT A concert, standing on the hillside, and he steps out of the crowd and starts dancing alone like he is a nut case? The camera pans over the crowd and you can see people laughing their heads off as this lone wolf just up and starts doing the Funky Trot. After a few minutes, a couple of guys from the crowd (who probably just wanted a laugh) step out and start dancing next to him. You can't tell if their goal is to embarrass Mr. Flashdance into giving up his dance routine or not, but regardless, there are now three guys dancing funky. The interesting part is within minutes the entire crowd on the hill is dancing with them. It only took one person who didn't care what he looked like to get the group into action. This is true leadership. At times, leaders must be willing to do whatever it takes to get others to join them.

I am always amazed at how infrequently vanity is discussed amongst my Christian friends. I believe this is because most people have an unrealistic definition of what vanity actually entails. The Merriam-Webster dictionary describes vanity as

"Inflated pride in oneself or one's appearance[17]." Note the second part of that definition—vanity also entails worrying about our image and what we look like to others. Too often we are afraid of what we will *appear* to be to other people, and what they will think about us.

I know that when it comes to working out, I fall into this trap. You know you need to work out because you are not taking care of your body the way you are supposed to, but who wants to work out with toned, bulging, gym rats when you don't like the way you look? Things are hanging and sagging … it doesn't look very appealing. Personally, I begin to perspire when I merely look at the sun. Regardless of the amount of fitness I do, I perspire enough to look like I just jumped out of the pool. Let's just say that when I am through, even my wife won't hug me.

Many people fall into this category and the result is that we tend to hide from the prying eyes we are convinced are looking at us. Turn on any infomercial and you will see evidence of this in the allegedly latest and greatest workout designed to be done "in the privacy of your own home." The real question is, "Are people really that concerned about you?"

In our vanity, we are so concerned about our appearance that we want to wait until we get into perfect shape before taking our workouts public. Hopefully, you can relate. In college, when I was in great shape, I scheduled all my runs during the daytime. Now, I tend to lean more toward the vampire schedule—late night or at the break of dawn. Once the sun starts peeking over the horizon, I am pushing it as hard as I can to get home. It is hilarious that we do this. Shouldn't we take the opposite approach? Why don't we let people see our reality so they are encouraged to follow suit?

[17] Merriam Webster Online Dictionary. "Vanity." Accessed July 29, 2022. https://www.merriam-webster.com/dictionary/vanity

I say this because the same rationale applies to our Christian walk. The global Church has a tendency to implicitly encourage the application of a member's faith mostly in the privacy of their own homes or church. Just count how many cars are parked at any given church on a Sunday morning. Chances are, in comparison to the total population, it is a good chunk of people. It should be no surprise considering over half of the United States identifies as Christian. Yet, where is this application of faith on Monday? Monday is when reality hits and you need faith the most. Less than twenty-four hours later, people become irate as their uniquely valuable time is wasted in traffic trying to get to work. Worse yet, there might be backstabbing around the coffee pot that somehow seems justified. Communication with spouses and children suddenly drops. Lustful eyes linger over some steamy internet ad—something we wouldn't dream of doing on Sunday …

Hopefully, you don't think I am pointing to anyone in particular out there. Unfortunately, at times the person I am describing is me.

We should be walking out our faith each and every day. John Piper says it like this,

> God created me—and you—to live with a single, all-embracing, all-transforming, passion— namely, a passion to glorify God by enjoying and displaying his supreme excellence in all the spheres of life. Enjoying and displaying are both crucial. If we try to display the excellence of God without joy in it, we will display a shell of hypocrisy and create scorn or legalism. But if we claim to enjoy his excellence and don't display it for others to see and admire, we deceive ourselves, because the mark of God-enthralled joy is to overflow and expand by extending itself into the hearts of

others. The wasted life is the life without a passion
for the supremacy of God in all things for the joy
of all peoples. [18]

Imagine if we reached out to the neighbor we don't know
very well? What if you knocked on their door and asked them to
grab some coffee in order to start a relationship? Or how different
would life look if we gave money to beggars just because they
asked? Would it be so out-of-the-box to say "Jesus loves you" to
every person to whom you handed your credit card?

What I believe Piper is saying is our motives should be all
about Christ and zero about us.

I am reminded of my friend, Bob Kulick, who could be called
a lot of things including entrepreneur, adventurer, leader, and
business executive. One thing you could never call him, however,
is a slouch. Bob tends to be one of those people who wakes up in
the morning and cannot wait to see what life has to offer him.
Name a river, he has probably boated on it. Name a mountain,
he has probably climbed it. I suppose one of the few things you
cannot call him is an astronaut but even this will change soon as
he is on a list to fly with Sir Richard Branson on Virgin Galactic.

It is safe to say that whatever Bob does in life, he is going
at it with gusto. From motorcycle rides to his professional life
where he was the CEO of CiCi's Pizza. Even in ministry, Kulick
is a go, go, go-getter. Instead of parlaying his successful career
in business to additional corporate roles, Bob used his success to
engage in ministries dedicated to discipleship. LGM is therefore
so blessed that he chose ours to be one of the ministries in which
he is engaged.

Surprisingly, Bob claims his success as a leader is not due to
his adventurer's spirit. Rather, he has been profitable in business

---

[18] Piper, John. *Don't Waste Your Life*. Crossway (May 16, 2003). Kindle.
Location 275-281.

and ministry because he is an engager and an includer of others. Certainly, we all (myself included) hope to absorb some of the energy Bob exudes. His motivation is contagious, yet Bob tends to discuss his actions in a way that includes the listener. He voices his passion for the things he is doing but in a subtle, infectious way. He invites you to experience the same passion he has. Participants in our various programs take comfort that Bob is out there with them. Regardless of the activity, he is leading by example.

In ministry, as in his life and career, Bob continues to be an includer. As Chair of the Board for LGM Ministries (LGM), he is ultimately responsible for the financial welfare and sustainability of our ministry. Rather than just focus on governance, though, Bob acts as an ambassador for our ministry. He often crisscrosses the country to visit partner ministries, or to help foster growth within certain states and institutions. Not only is he inviting local individuals, groups, and congregations to get engaged, but Bob is often inviting others to join him on his travels.

At LGM events, like our annual graduation festival in Louisiana called Returning Hearts Celebration, Bob will arrive with a group of newcomers that he invited to participate in the three-day event working with incarcerated men and women. Bob wants to *show* people what he is involved in. Although I would love to think that all the people I have met through Bob have been called to "prison ministry," I honestly believe some are called to be involved in whatever Bob invites them to. They know his commitment and passion and desire to be a part of it.

Since much of his background has been at 30,000 feet as a corporate executive, Bob also sits on other Christian non-profit boards dedicated to discipleship and education. One of the many things I have come to appreciate about him is his ability to break down organizational walls and encourage ministries to work together. His way of doing this comes back to invitation. He invites us to engage the other ministries of which he is a part, and vice versa.

In contrast, at times I am ashamed of myself for worrying about what it would look like to share and openly live out my faith a hundred percent of the time. I am ashamed because Jesus Christ, who was fully God when He walked the Earth (and still is), allowed Himself to be supremely humiliated on my behalf. I find that it isn't so much I miss opportunities, rather I am simply *scared* to act. You see, as with my workouts, even when I am trying, I am afraid of what people will say or think. In many ways, we are just like the Pharisees; they were filled with zeal and by worldly standards were on fire for God. Yet Christ warns in Matthew 7:21 that "[21] "Not everyone who says to me, 'Lord, Lord,' will enter the kingdom of heaven, but the one who does the will of my Father who is in heaven." It certainly appears that those who are unashamedly willing to do His complete will are those who please God most.

To fully embrace the relationship God wants to have for us, we need to be willing to lay down everything we have for Him. We tend to focus on whether we are giving Him our time, our talents, and our resources but I believe the biggest hindrance to our progress is the unwillingness to lay down our *image*. Remember, it only takes one person who is willing to risk it all to motivate the group to join them. Like Bob Kulick, if we are able to lay down our vanity, not worry about what people will think of us no matter what pinnacles of success we've attained, and give it all to Christ each and every day, people will naturally be encouraged to join us. This week, let's be such a leader.

I want to leave you with a thought from the book *Talent Is Overrated*[19] by Geoff Colvin. Colvin breaks down the difference between practice (which can sometimes be a waste of time) and deliberate practice (seeking improvement in key areas). The two chapters from which I gained the most were *Applying the Principles*

[19] Colvin, Geoffrey. *Talent Is Overrated: What Really Separates World-Class Performers from Everybody Else.* New York: Portfolio/Penguin, 2018.

to Our Lives and *Applying the Principles to Our Organization.* Here are a few key points:

a. Understand that each person in the organization is not just doing a job, but is also being stretched and grown.
b. Find ways to develop leaders within their jobs.
c. Encourage leaders to be active in their communities.
d. Understand the critical roles of teachers and feedback.
e. Identify promising performers early.
f. Understand that people development works best through inspiration, not authority.
g. Invest significant time, money, and energy developing people.
h. Make leadership development a part of the culture.

Keep in mind it is never fun to run the race alone. God didn't design us this way. In all areas of ministry, Christ spoke of community. Like Jesus, like the apostle Paul, and like Bob Kulick, we should never run alone. Great leaders always encourage others to join them. This effort will not only create success in your work life, but it will also help build Kingdom success which is far more impactful.

SEVEN

Quicken the Pace

I HAVEN'T QUITE WORKED OUT WHY, BUT I PREFER EXERCISING IN water far more than on land. Maybe it's because the older I become the greater my level of buoyancy. It may also be the idea that quitting isn't an option. When I'm running, the opportunity to just stop and say "That's enough!" is always there, but when I'm swimming, if I stop I sink, even with my recently elevated buoyancy.

In an attempt to become proficient in this form of exercise, and because I enjoy it, I used to meet with a master's swimming group for swim practice three times a week, where our coach put us through our paces. Allow me to provide a clear picture of the group: we were comprised of a collection of adults of various ages who generally came from some form of swimming discipline. Each swimmer had their lane in which they practice at a competitive level to prepare them for any meet. Then there was me. I was relegated to the far lane for remedial training, and it would be some time, if ever, that I needed to worry about participating in a swim meet. This, nonetheless, did not deter the coach from working me hard. As we progressed through the practice, he pushed me harder, faster, and longer, all in an effort to build my endurance and increase my speed.

If you are like me, the hardest part of any exercise tends to be at the beginning or the end. When I start exercising, I have a hard time settling into a steady pace. No matter what the task, my body will generally start to feel the initial stress of whatever exercise I'm engaged in, and it will begin to revolt. It might be my old joints starting to creak at the impact or maybe a little cramp creeping into my side. Once I'm up to speed and cruising, though, I begin to find a groove that works. My breathing is in sync and my body works efficiently at keeping the pace.

Leaving Our Comfort Zone

Finding a groove during exercise may make the task a little easier and more pleasant to perform, but in our Christian walks, however, the Lord doesn't want us falling into a routine. Rather, He wants us to continue striving for Him, and generally, this means pushing us out of our comfort zone, which entails picking up the pace. Just like in a physical race, our body and our mind are going to provide negative feedback. They will be none too happy to be pushed outside of their related comfort zones.

We know our bodies and we know what we can do. We also think we know what is best, but the Lord tells us through scripture that He knows the plans He has for us (Jeremiah 29:11) and they are ultimately good. Like any great coach, He knows what we can take, and the levels to which we can be pushed. We have to learn to trust that He knows what He is doing when He dials it up a bit.

God has, after all, coached some great leadership champions before us. Take Moses for example. He was a known murderer who wasn't comfortable speaking in front of a group, yet the Lord wanted his all from Moses. Even though Moses complained, the Lord still motivated Him to pick up the pace because that is what good coaches do. How about David? As a shepherd, the Lord asked him to elevate his game and to take on the giant warrior, Goliath. David was obedient to the Lord's call and rose to prominence, eventually finding himself in the king's presence. For most, this would have been the pinnacle of a career, but as far as it concerned David, the Lord still knew that David had a lot more to offer. The challenges increased until David cried out in the Psalms as King Saul pursued him, yet the Lord continued to push David at an increasing pace all the way to his final day.

In our humanity, it is natural for us to hesitate in leaving our comfort zone. Remember the old saying about upsetting the apple cart? We're in the zone, everything is flowing, why would we want to change things and mess it up? Situations for improvement arise every day and we need to be alert and open to hearing God's voice—He just may be telling us to pick up the pace. Perhaps the Lord is calling you toward a full-time position outside of your industry? With college to pay for or retirement to fund, you force the idea out of your head. It could be He is prompting you to get involved with the single-parent child down the street, but you chalk it up to self-conceived inner dialog. Besides, you have your hands full with your own kids. He may put offering up pro bono administrative help at the local shelter on your heart, but that might mean cutting down your work week, which could affect your chances at the next promotion.

The point is if it's of God—and you need to learn to know if He is the one asking you to pick up the pace—then you need to trust Him. The Lord will be there to help you when you need it. This is what He tells us in His Word: "You have given me the shield of your salvation, and your right hand supported me, and your gentleness made me great" (Psalm 18:35), and "God, the Lord, is my strength; he makes my feet like the deer's; he makes me tread on my high places" (Habakkuk 3:19). If we listen for His voice and are obedient to His direction, the Lord will use these opportunities to pick up the pace in our spiritual races, in order to draw us closer to Him.

It's interesting to note that often, the obstacles facing us which seem to hamper our pace, unexpectedly turn out to be a means to *quicken* our pace. An example of this occurred in November 2018 when up to that point, LGM's international team, directed by Dan Bostrom, had been wrestling with how to reach a dozen countries in Africa. We wanted to make our training available to introduce and facilitate the Malachi Dads program.

It was impractical to bring the leaders to the United States because attempting to get everyone in a central location would have been difficult with vastly different schedules, time zones, and travel implications. Despite our materials often being translated into the language of the home country, we still had to overcome language barriers. The biggest problem, though, was the cost. It would be near-impossible to underwrite the cost of getting these partners to the U.S., not to mention the logistical nightmare it would present.

After praying about the challenge we had what we thought at the time was an epiphany. We thought *Why not take advantage of the students' proximity to one another and the lower travel costs in Africa?* Instead of trying to bring the students to us, we would go to *them* with regional training. So that's exactly what we did. In November 2018, Dan, his wife, Marylin, and I were overjoyed to facilitate training in Kigali, Rwanda. What made the training so special is there were approximately twenty individuals present representing twelve countries from the continent of Africa. Today we have a thriving ministry operating in these countries, with each of these individuals serving as ministry leaders to the incarcerated in their respective home countries.

After completing the sessions, Dan and his team high-fived one another thankful that God had provided the wisdom to go this route. They had been open to the Lord's direction and indeed, although challenging, the Lord had quickened the pace and they were obedient. We had been given an exciting, successful new paradigm and could settle into a routine for a while. This would be the way we do training for the foreseeable future ... or so we thought. By August of 2020, travel bans and COVID protocols made it virtually impossible to organize any in-person events. When what would have worked perfectly with the same method, we now had to figure out how to train another group of ministry partners, this time representing countries in Central and South America.

The obstacle hindering our forward momentum—lockdowns and travel bans—brought about another acceleration—we had to rapidly explore avenues of videoconferencing technology for training we had not previously used *en masse*. Using this new medium, we organized a three-day training event, spread over the course of three weeks, also making the training available to two of our global partners. By God's grace, we had over *three hundred* people register for the training, representing a host of countries across five continents! Talk about quickening the pace!

Though the LGM's international team had already quickened their pace in this matter, God continued stretching them way beyond what they thought they could achieve.

The takeaway here is that ours is a race of *endurance*. When we quicken our pace it is not to finish the race sooner, but rather, by adjusting our pace we broaden our capacity to run the race as efficiently as we can. The Message Translation puts it this way: "So don't sit around on your hands! No more dragging your feet! Clear the path for long-distance runners so no one will trip and fall, so no one will step in a hole and sprain an ankle. Help each other out. And run for it!' (Hebrews 12: 12-13—MSG).

Quickening the pace in our spiritual walk or ministry will almost certainly thrust us out of our comfort zone because, in pushing ourselves a little farther or a little harder, we might push ourselves into some unsettling areas of vulnerability. This is okay; sometimes we are at our strongest when we are vulnerable. Brene Brown, the bestselling author, and speaker explains it like this in her book *The Gifts of Imperfection*:

Embracing our vulnerabilities is risky but not
nearly as dangerous as giving up on love and
belonging and joy—the experiences that make
us the most vulnerable. Only when we are brave
enough to explore the darkness will we discover
the infinite power of our light.[20]

God-Ordained Possibilities

Of course, as with any race, picking up the pace can be
difficult at times. It may be uncomfortable because we've tried
something different before and failed, or worse, we feel we are
already giving everything we have. It's important to know your
abilities, but we also need to be aware that the grace of God can
increase our capacity to do His will in ways beyond anything we
thought we could achieve.

In the Old Testament, we see examples of how God used the
ministries and lives of people in ways they never dreamed possible.
In some cases, as with Moses and Gideon, they even pushed back
and resisted the task God set before them because they didn't
feel adequate for the job. In the New Testament, we witness the
extraordinary feats Paul was able to perform through Christ Who
strengthened him (Philippians 4:13), and the courage provided to
Stephen as he rebuked the Sanhedrin.

Much like a perfectly hit baseball or a perfect golf swing,
extraordinary momentum is developed when we find the sweet
spot in our ministry and in our lives. This sweet spot is found when
we are fully living out the call of Christ in our lives. The power,
distance, and trajectory of what we can do in Christ significantly
outperforms anything we thought possible on our own.

---

[20] Brene Brown. *The Gifts of Imperfection: Let Go of Who You Think You're
Supposed to Be and Embrace Who You Are.* Center City, Minn.: Hazelden.
2010. Pg 6.

One person who gets this is an exceptional Kingdom worker named Leah Howard. Leah, formerly incarcerated in Ohio, found her calling in a life in Christ. I encourage you to view her astounding video testimony on LGM's website (http://lifelineglobal.org). Desiring to be a godly woman and mother, Leah enrolled, then graduated from LGM's Hannah's Gift Program. While her life was transformed by the power of the Holy Spirit during her time behind bars, God desired more from Leah.

Upon being released from prison, Leah joined a church with a significant outreach program at the facility from which she had been released. Less than a year after her release, Leah approached the church leadership with a call to start a prison ministry. Leah knew that women who shared a similar story to hers needed someone to walk beside them, teach them, and disciple them to live life in a new way. With her church's support, she was able to pick up the pace of her ministry. She went from being discipled to fostering discipleship relationships with hundreds of others.

Today Leah is a pivotal member of the Board of Directors of LGM. She also serves as the Outreach Director at the church she attends, and has been instrumental in fostering the growth of other ministries in under-resourced areas of Dayton, Ohio. Leah's testimony proves that when God calls us to quicken the pace nothing is impossible, and she continues to remain open to God's voice and to increase the pace whenever God ordains it.

The Lord can turn obstacles into opportunities to quicken our pace, but what this means is that we must seek His voice, then be open to, and embrace any change in our lives and ministries. Our ministries are grown by allowing God to stretch our capabilities to overcome obstacles we haven't faced before. This also teaches us to rely on the guidance of the Holy Spirit and to trust the Lord when our course changes. Of course, since changing courses is clearly a method the Lord uses, it certainly helps to be prepared for that eventuality. In the next chapter, we will discuss how to best be prepared if the course changes.

EIGHT

Be Prepared If the Course Changes

AMERICANS TEND TO BE ENAMORED WITH OBSTACLE COURSES. I think it started in the 1970s when families crowded around the television set to watch Battle of the Network Stars. If you have never seen the show it pitted famous actors against one another in a variety of athletic events. In the 80s we saw the show American Gladiator where television used a similar concept by designing changing athletic courses that became increasingly difficult. Contestants ran various, extremely challenging gauntlets while battling giant, well-muscled opponents.

The shows and obstacle courses have continued to evolve, but have never lost their appeal. American Ninja is the current rage and doesn't appear to be losing steam after many seasons. This has also spawned new business models like The Spartan Race and One Tough Mudder which have been created for individuals and teams to compete in ever-changing, ultra-competitive races. Certainly part of the appeal is the physical challenge, yet the greatest thrill seems to come from the variety of challenges dreamed up by the course designers. Can the contestants run a little farther or faster? Can they jump higher? Can they persevere?

Mention ministry in this dynamic, however, and what seems attractive gets turned upside down. Where in athletic pursuits (pick your sport) people enjoy rising to the challenge, in our faith walks and ministry our approach to change is generally very different.

Typically, when the course begins to change we resist it wholeheartedly. Sometimes this is likely because we have grown comfortable with where we are in life. We bought into the mantra, "If it ain't broke, don't fix it." We enjoy the patterns and the consistencies in life and we steer clear of anything that might disrupt it. How then will we ever be challenged to stretch ourselves?

I believe our hesitation to change is due to fear of the unknown. In fact, many times we are willing to accept the known regardless of how painful or destructive it is, as it gives us a false sense of peace. *The devil you know* ... as the saying goes. Yet God did not design us to remain at the same level. He created His children to be continually changing; growing and improving. The very definition of life is growth, is it not? A baby that remained unchanging in the womb would be considered dead. Plants grow, babies grow, and even the cells in our body continue to regenerate. The landscape around us is shaped by the weather. Technology transforms how we communicate and become informed. Economies move up and down regardless of the type of government.

Whether we like it or not, change is here to stay.

I love what John Piper said in his book *Let the Nation be Glad,* "So we must not water down the call to suffer. We must not domesticate the New Testament teaching on affliction and persecution just because our lives are so smooth.[21]" I am convinced our lives will become increasingly "unsmooth" if we resist any changes in events or landscape.

---

[21] Piper, John. *Let the Nations be Glad.* p.76. Baker Academics Grand Rapids, MI, 2003.

Some people hate change yet it is an unflinching phenomenon, and often our success and our failure can be rooted in our response to change. It is not a question of *how* a situation will change; rather, it's *when* will it happen, and determining how you will adapt could be the difference between success and failure. Again, as in athletic endeavors, it comes down to perseverance. If you ever believe it's getting too tough to adapt to any changes, consider Hebrews 13:12-14:

> [12] So Jesus also suffered outside the gate in order to sanctify the people through his own blood. [13] Therefore let us go to him outside the camp and bear the reproach he endured. [14] For here we have no lasting city, but we seek the city that is to come.

All too often, however, people repeatedly find themselves unable to adapt to alternating circumstances. In developing their plans, they do a very effective job of setting realistic goals. In many cases, they might develop identifiable metrics to help measure their progress toward reaching their goal. Yet, with the Lord, we often have no understanding of where His race may take us. I am reminded of a quote by the Roman emperor and stoic Marcus Aurelius: "The impediment to action advances action. What stands in the way becomes the way." What he means is that when you resist change too long, complacency becomes your way of life.

If you are a fan of organizational management author Jim Collins, you are probably familiar with the acronym BHAG. It stands for "Big Hairy Audacious Goal" and refers to the bold strategic planning and development of organizations. At LGM, we serve a God for Whom no goals are too big. That's why I stretched our organizational goal in 2022 to reach *22,000 incarcerated students!*

God has shown our team that even in the throes of Covid, He can and will do great things. In 2020 and 2021, LGM programming looked extremely bleak. At the start of the pandemic over ninety-percent of our programming was shut down worldwide. Even so, God used this as an opportunity to open new avenues for reaching incarcerated men and women and their families. Through our video projects, we reached twenty-five percent more students in 2021 than the average of previous years. This is because we refused to resist change but instead relied on God to show us how to adapt. What followed was an *increase* in LGM's fruit.

At the time of this writing we are in mid-2022, but I know we can more than double the number of incarcerated men and women who are positively impacted. With the help of our partners, we can add even more Malachi Dads and see an increase in Hannah's Gift. Can you imagine *22,000* incarcerated people's lives changed? The expectation is that these 22,000 individuals would reach another 22,000 parents who are not incarcerated! More importantly, the trajectory of a minimum of 44,000 children would have their lives forever changed as their mother or father is guided by the Holy Spirit to restore the family. Realistically, we expect to impact over 100,000 people in 2022. This is all because we yielded to the Holy Spirit's guidance as global change impacted us.

The story of Job is a similar one. Things were progressing along pretty well for him until they weren't. According to scripture Job had a wife, many children, as well as enormous wealth. Job's life likely wasn't like one of the mega-wealthy families you see on today's reality television shows; his family appeared to be close and have great relationships. Job was the kind of guy you couldn't help but like. He strove to do things the right way and had many friends and people who loved him. Most importantly, Job was a man of faith who gave credit to his heavenly Father when credit was due. The book of Job describes him as a man who was blameless and upright (Job 1:1). He would spend each and every day in prayer for his family, offering burnt offerings in their name. Until one day, Satan attacked, and it was stolen from him.

In less than twenty-four hours, Job lost his children, his health, and his wealth. I can't even imagine this. I have heard of modern stories where people's lives are turned upside down, but certainly nothing to this extent. One day Job's life is constant and going great. The next day it is all gone. Even in times of war, one generally has an inkling of what might happen. Not for Job through; it was just *bam!* and life had completely changed. If this does not send a shiver down your spine, I don't know what will.

In his suffering, Job cried out to the Lord. It is obvious to Job there has been some sort of huge clerical mistake in Heaven. In his agony, Job has the nerve to blame the Lord and justify himself. Eventually, man oh man, does the Lord let him have it. The Lord says to Job (my paraphrasing) "Who are you to justify yourself over Me? Do you have an inkling of how I designed this world? Are you aware of how I created the stars in the sky? Are you that sure you are more righteous than Me?"

Despite Job's blithe self-righteousness, and strong (if understandable) resistance to change, God has mercy on him and blesses Job with twice as much as he had before. We see the intent the Lord had for Job when Satan sought to attack him and test his faithfulness. Although God never tests us with evil, if we leave a door open for Satan to attack us as Job did with his self-righteousness, God may use it for our ultimate benefit. Resisting such change, however, especially when we desperately need God's mercy as Job did, is a very bad idea.

In a contrasting story, I recently had a chance to be a part of the ninetieth birthday celebration of Dr. Gene Getz. Among the significant roles Dr. Getz has had are best-selling author, theologian, pastor, and church planter, so it stands to reason that people from all over the country joined to honor the man and his career. Christian heavyweights like Tony Evans and Chuck Swindoll spoke of the impact Dr. Getz has had on them. June

Hunt even serenaded him with a guitar-led hymn, and author Jerry B. Jenkins (of the famed *Left Behind* series) and Moody Bible Institute President, Mark Jobe, were there to offer congratulations.

Dr. Getz is a man who epitomizes the person who is prepared when the course changes. For over fifty years, he has been engaged in running the race, yet during that time, God has sought a myriad of different things from him. We read in Dr. Getz's biography that,

> His early career was spent in the world of academics, first as professor for thirteen years at Moody Bible Institute, then as professor for eight years at Dallas Theological Seminary. While teaching at DTS, he was challenged to confront the disillusionment that grew out of the era of the '60s and early '70s. After many dynamic class sessions and interaction with his students, Gene wrote *Sharpening the Focus of the Church*. This book led to his launching of the original Fellowship Bible Church in 1972, starting a movement that continues today in the form of hundreds of Fellowship and Fellowship-type churches around the world. Gene's efforts over the years have directly impacted the lives of millions of individuals. He has written more than 60 books most of which grew out of his experience as a pastor. *The Measure of a Man* has become a classic and has never gone out of print in more than forty years.

Although being a leader in each field, Dr. Getz was open to the changing landscape God presented to him. The course changed when Dr. Getz went from being a sought-after academic to being a renowned author and then he progressed to becoming a church planter. Rather than just focus on his own success in establishing a church, he adapted again to a course change in leading an entire *movement* of churches. Through the grace of God, LGM benefitted when God put another path in Dr. Getz's life.

When he was invited to visit inmates in prison, Dr. Getz saw the value that the teachings of his book *The Measure of a Man* could have on restoring men to being the godly leader they were created to be. He graciously reworked his material to create *Heart of Man*—a two-part curriculum used by LGM as part of its Malachi Dads program for incarcerated men.

Continuing from his biography we see other development as a result of the change in Dr. Getz's life:

> After transitioning from his role as Senior Pastor more than ten years ago, the Life Essentials Study Bible (Broadman-Holman, 2011) is now the centerpiece of his ministry. Its unique format includes 1500 supracultural "principles to live by," each with a QR code providing access to a total of 250 total hours of video teaching.

The sales from these Bibles are reinvested in free Bibles for men and women in under-resourced areas. His ministry provides a study Bible for every inmate graduate of LGM's Malachi Dads and Hannah's Gift programs.

At over ninety years old, Dr. Gene Getz continues to run his race with endurance and adaptation. Even at his advanced age, he remains open and prepared for course changes. To likewise be prepared for when our road changes, we only need to look to the great Orchestrator of Life, to determine our next steps. Look at what scripture says about knowing the future; when questioned about when He would return to Earth, Jesus responded with, "But concerning that day and hour no one knows, not even the angels of heaven, nor the Son, but the Father only," (Matthew 24:36).

We can be assured God knows our future and we, therefore, need to trust Him and His ways. We can build this trust by including the future in our prayer respective lives.

When considering change, I'll leave you with what 1 Corinthians 2:11-12 tells us,

> [11] For who knows a person's thoughts except the spirit of that person, which is in him? So also no one comprehends the thoughts of God except the Spirit of God. [12] Now we have received not the spirit of the world, but the Spirit who is from God, that we might understand the things freely given us by God.

This profound passage means that the very Spirit of God lives within us, so doesn't it make sense He can be relied upon to guide us and lead us through every period of change and growth? I promise you it does.

So now we know, not only the necessity of adapting to change but how to rely on God to do so. Let's take a look at the next, exciting and long-awaited step which is learning how to finish the race by envisioning the finish line.

NINE

Envision the Finish Line

So now finish doing it as well,
so that your readiness in desiring it
may be matched by your completing it
out of what you have.
2 Corinthians 8:11

MOST OF WHAT I HAVE WRITTEN IN *FINDING YOUR PACE* I LEARNED
by *being* in the race. Primarily I have learned that our spiritual race
truly is a marathon, and most often not an easy one. It certainly
is, however, rewarding even just to know I'm being obedient to
God's calling on my life. In my spiritual race, I use these lessons
on endurance, planning, and staying the course, on a daily basis.
Many such lessons from the physical races I participate in have
helped me, and one of the most important of these has been a bike
ride known as Critical Mass.

You may be familiar with the name, but it has different
meanings depending on the city you are in. For Los Angeles, it's
nothing more than a fun ride with a little over three thousand
fellow Angelinos. The police are out in force and block off the
entire route for the riders' safety. While there are still a fair
amount of small accidents, for the most part, it is a great way to get
out into the sun, be around other people, and enjoy some exercise.

Los Angeles and the surrounding cities have their share of hills, and sure, the hills aren't the Alps over which the riders of the Tour de France find themselves navigating, but they still can get you quite winded. On an average Critical Mass ride, I can find myself riding anywhere from thirty to forty miles, and for a guy like me, that's a long haul. I start off strong, but about twenty miles in I suddenly hit a wall. The hills exhaust me, and the constant shifts the in pace of speeding up and slowing down, common to large group rides, takes its toll as well. At certain points during the race, it takes all the strength I have left not to call my wife, Amy, to come and fetch me. I want to just pull over, sit on a curb, and wait for a ride home. What I do to get me through these brutal periods is I simply imagine myself cruising toward the finish line.

The organizers of the race vary the course every month but the finish is always at Sunset and Western in Los Angeles. As my lungs heave and my thighs burn, in high resolution I envision myself riding down Sunset Strip. All of the festive revelers line the street, out for a good time on a warm Friday night. I focus my thoughts away from my body's pain, zeroing in on that finish line. This only gets me through a quarter mile. I have to really start painting the picture in my mind … people waving, cheering me on, children's eyes wide with awe, the celebratory sounds and sights of the famous Sunset Strip. This gets me through the next mile … I see my beautiful wife beaming from ear to eye, arms wide open at the finish line … that gets me through the following one … I zero in on the tape … how sweet the relief and joy of victory if I can only hang on … that gets me through the mile after that, and mile by mile goes the fight to draw my focus away from the suffering until I can hardly believe I actually see the real finish line like a dream before me.

Someone who knows what it's like to maintain the course by envisioning the finish line is a runner called Louie Zamperini, a remarkable person and a true Kingdom warrior. If you don't know Zamperini's story I strongly suggest reading his biography by Laura Hillenbrand called *Unbroken: A World War II Story of Survival, Resilience, and Redemption*[22] or even watching the movie of the same name. Spoiler alert! The following is a very brief synopsis. Hillenbrand begins Zamperini's life story as a small boy in Southern California who uses running as a way to escape the difficulties he encounters in his youth. This serves him well as he grows older, with Louie becoming one of the fastest middle-distance runners in the world, competing in the 5,000-meter track event at the 1936 Berlin Olympics. At the time, many believed he would be the first runner to break the four-minute mile.

World War II erupts before he can reach the world stage again, and Louie finds himself going from a college track star at USC to an officer in the US Army Air Corps as a bombardier. His plane is promptly shot down over the Pacific during his very first tour, but God spares Louie's life. He is, however, adrift on a small raft with two of his crew, on sixty-four million square miles of ocean. With no food or water, they eat raw seagulls they manage to catch landing on the raft. As he was fighting to stay alive, Louie calls out to God, pleading to be rescued. He makes a deal with the Lord vowing to give his life to Christ if he is rescued.

Louie ends up setting a world record, but it is for the longest time spent in a lifeboat before being rescued. Even so, Louie's trials were just beginning as Louie and his crew are taken prisoner by a Japanese military vessel. Instead of getting the chance to recover, Louie is thrown into a prison camp where he is starved, tortured, and worked to the point of death. Still, Louie keeps striving to live one more day, envisioning his return to the beautiful life he once had. His training as a runner taught him to endure discomfort and pain because Olympic athletes are wired a little differently to most of us. Their single-minded determination to focus on the finish

---

[22] Hillenbrand, Laura. 2014. *Unbroken: A World War II Story of Survival, Resilience and Redemption*. New York: Randon Hause Trade Paperbacks.

line is something from which we all could learn. Louie never lost sight of the finish line.

Louie's dogged perseverance paid off when, years later, he was eventually rescued from the prisoner of war camp. Imagine the fanfare when he returned to the US—an Olympic hero most had written off as dead. His own family didn't even know he was still alive. Louie was immediately thrust back into the limelight; into what would have been rock-star status back then. Everyone wanted him at their speaking engagements, and he received numerous calls to make appearances at various functions. The question on everyone's mind was whether he would begin racing again.

Although Louie envisioned the finish line all through his ordeal, his perception of what the finish line would be, and the expectation God had for him, turned out to be vastly different. The fame and celebrity so soon after being a prisoner of war ended up being too much for him. The pressure he faced while dealing with the demons of being a rescued prisoner of war had a dramatic effect on the man. Alcoholism took over and his life tail spun out of control. His marriage and family were deeply affected.

I am convinced the reason for this tragic twist after such a struggle is because he no longer had a finish line. What I mean is, the finish line of returning to the life he once knew sort of happened and sort of didn't. Louie had changed. Life had changed. And the finish line was not all he had dreamed it to be. Instead of adjusting his lifestyle and heart to find the greater finish line, he became distracted by worldly fame and everything going on around him, and Louie lost his legendary focus.

How many times does this happen to us, especially on our spiritual journey? We focus on the things of this world and lose sight of what awaits us in the next life, or even in the phase of ministry. Paul didn't allow himself to be distracted by opposition to his ministry or the appeal of an easy life; he was always focused on the finish line and nothing could deter him from getting there. Paul knew exactly what to expect at the end of his race saying,

> [7] I have fought the good fight, I have finished the race, I have kept the faith. [8] Henceforth there is laid up for me the crown of righteousness, which the Lord, the righteous judge, will award to me on that day, and not only to me but also to all who have loved his appearing. 2 Timothy 4:7-8

We really must cultivate the same level of focus as Paul displays here. Our everyday lives and our ministries are not separate, meaning it is imperative we remain focused on the righteous judge, Jesus Christ. In his book *Knowing Jesus Through the Old Testament*[23], Christopher Wright correctly states that we are to put God first in all things. He adds that secondly, we are to love people more than things, and third, we need to address needs more than rights (pages 211-213).

These sound like three simple rules, but we must remember that the evil one is striving to get us off course. In fact, he would like nothing better than to see us quit. He distracts us in various ways in an effort to keep our attention focused on the here and now, instead of on the Kingdom. This may be through the way we entertain ourselves, how we behave behind closed doors, the "toys" he convinces us we must have, or the manner in which we handle our finances. To maintain a clear vision of the finish line, a Kingdom mindset is imperative. When we sustain a Kingdom mindset as Paul did, we are able to persevere through all life throws at us.

Louie Zamperini may have lost his focus but God had not forgotten the promise Louie made while drifting on the raft at sea. God is faithful and He still had a plan for Louie's life. While

---

[23] Wright, Christopher J H. 2014. *Knowing Jesus through the Old Testament.* Downers Grove, Illinois: Ivp Academic, An Imprint Of Intervarsity Press.

Louie battled his demons, a young preacher by the name of Billy Graham decided to hold his first revival service in Los Angeles. Louie's wife attended the service and made the decision to give her life to Christ. After much urging, Louie agreed to attend a different event with her, but he was still very much blinded by his lifestyle and struggles, and Louie could not find peace. Only after a second visit to one of the services was Louie ready for God to reveal Himself, and remind him of the promise he had made while floating in the ocean. Louie's eyes were opened and he immediately saw the true finish line ahead of him. From that day forward, Louie kept his eyes on the finish line of his upward call and devoted his life to the Kingdom of Heaven.

Closer to home, I have personally had the honor of serving with someone who never took his eyes off the finish line, either. I met Steve Weinberg on the rodeo grounds of Angola State Prison in Louisiana. For any unfamiliar with Angola Prison, it is commonly referred to as the deadliest prison in America. Steve was participating in LGM's graduation event called Returning Hearts Celebration. Never one to be idle, Steve used his time at the celebration to interact with men who most people refer to as murderers, rapists, and thieves. Steve knew of God's restoration power and saw these men only as Christian brothers. In Steve, I witnessed someone who promptly heard the call from Christ to become extensively engaged in this ministry. As a man of action, Steve quickly joined the Board of LGM, anxious to be involved in reaching the forgotten.

The most astonishing part of Steve's story is that he had *already* lived a life full of service to others. He earned his M.D. from the University of Iowa, training at UT Southwestern Medical Center. After successfully practicing as a general surgeon, Steve began his second career as an attorney, studying abroad at Oxford and earning his law degree from SMU. He taught at Tarrant County College and worked in real estate development, oil and gas, ranching, as well as in private equity. Steve had also served in the U.S. Air Force as Chief of Surgical Services at Ramey Air Force Base. Later, he was appointed by President George W. Bush as Associate Director and Medical Director of the Peace Corps. Add to this Steve's other government appointments, the fact that he was a long-time church member in Texas and Colorado, was past president of his local Rotary Club and completed mission trips to Honduras, Haiti, and Africa. Put plainly, his life was a continual service to others.

He could easily have retreated to the golf course and enjoyed an easy life of retirement, but his focus was on his calling. His vision was split between the need in the areas he was called to serve and that of carrying out his calling to the end. In other words, he maintained his vision of the finish line. Steve's ability to do so much was certainly influenced by his God-given skills and capability. More importantly, though, it was fostered by his ability to envision the finish line. Through his faith life, Steve knew his time on Earth was temporary and sought diligently to hear the words, "Well done good and faithful servant."

I am happy to say that Steve Weinberg reached the finish line he envisioned. He passed away in 2021, and those who knew him will attest to a faith-filled life of whirlwind activity. At LGM, we certainly miss his leadership on our Board of Directors and his ministry to families of the incarcerated, but we have all befitted from knowing him and witnessing his example of living for the finish line.

Search Your Heart

Several times I have emphasized that the Lord has a plan for your life; He has provided all you need to fulfill that call—to run the race—and among others, has promised the ultimate reward of eternal life with Him at the finish line. It is up to you to stay focused, use what you have been given, and not get sidetracked, either by glory in your achievements, or the obstacles in your way. You need to be on the lookout for anything that might lead you off the course to the finish—to catch the little foxes that spoil the vineyards of your life and ministry (Song of Solomon 2:15). I promise you that God has a calling on your life, but that doesn't automatically mean you are assured of making it to the finish line. King Saul is a clear example of this.

Saul had everything needed to become a great king in Israel. From a natural perspective, he was head-and-shoulders taller than anyone else in the country, good-looking, came from a wealthy family, and had "presence" in a crowd (1 Samuel 9:1-2). More importantly, he was chosen and anointed to be king by God. At first, Saul was obedient to his calling and God ensured Saul's success on the battlefield where the kingdom of Israel was renewed and revitalized. Saul's success, however, caused him to lose sight of his calling and his first love. He became arrogant, self-assured, and too impatient to wait on the Lord (1 Samuel 13:12). Saul lost the opportunity to have his kingdom established over Israel forever (1 Samuel 13:13). In a dramatic unfolding of events, this promise was subsequently given to David, who lived his life as a man after God's own heart (1 Samuel 13:14).

We need to be aware that the enemy doesn't only try to hinder our race with external obstacles. All too often we are caught out by something within ourselves. David, who was well aware of his many faults, prayed, "²³ Search me, O God, and know my heart! Try me and know my thoughts! ²⁴ And see if there be any grievous way in me, and lead me in the way everlasting" (Psalm 139: 23-24). David knew how to keep his eyes on the everlasting reward of the finish line, trusting God to lead him to the end.

In John 14:6 Jesus told us clearly He is the way to the Father, meaning if we keep our eyes on Him we won't lose our way to the finish line. When He ascended, Jesus sent the Holy Spirit to help guide us when we are in danger of straying from the course. We would do well to echo David's prayer daily, asking the Holy

Spirit to reveal anything within that weighs us down or leads us away from the finish line.

Most races are run for a reward, be it the satisfaction of simply having exercised, or the acclaim of the world, yet it is good to consider what the rewards are for the spiritual race in which we are running. Possibly more important, should we be running simply for the reward? In the next chapter, we will discuss the various, exciting aspects of receiving your reward and see exactly what we've been promised.

TEN

Receive Your Reward

AS YOU HAVE READ THIS BOOK, PERHAPS YOU STILL MAY NOT BE convinced about this call to action. Maybe you enjoyed the stories, and you even empathize with some of the characters who have had their lives touched, but feel you either have your own race to run or don't share my belief that you are called by God for a specific purpose. For some, this material simply may not have inspired you to get up out of the pew and live your faith day in and day out. You are satisfied with your walk that entails showing up for church services on Sunday (and even possibly Wednesday evenings). When asked about your faith, you are willing to tell people that you are a Christian, but you are not surprised when the person responds, "Really?" If this is the case, there is a crucial motivating aspect you may be overlooking; the mindboggling reward that could be yours.

I'm not saying this should be a movement that is paraded before others for reward from man. Both Jesus and Paul remind us to be humble with our words and deeds, serving the Lord just as diligently in isolation as in the public eye (Matthew 6:1, Colossians 3:23-24). If any of us are struggling to accept the importance and timeliness of this call to action, could it be because we have not allowed the Holy Spirit to persuade our hearts? Are we just talking a good game yet our walks don't match the words that come out of our mouths?

Please hear me; I'm not judging anyone. I truly want the very best for you, but like the workout metaphors I've used from my own life, to make any worthy change requires some straight talk and some disruption to one's comfort zone. Heaven forbid we become like the church of Laodicea, of whom God warns in Revelation 3:15-16, "¹⁵ 'I know your works: you are neither cold nor hot. Would that you were either cold or hot! ¹⁶ So, because you are lukewarm, and neither hot nor cold, I will spit you out of my mouth." This church and its members were obviously not in the race; they were comfortable sitting on the bench. They were happy in the crowd, watching the other runners go by. They weren't among the group that outright rejected God; they were probably even cheering the runners on. Still, they were simply not willing to partake in a more dynamic relationship with their God and be obedient to His call to *get in the race.*

Jesus provides even greater clarity and an even sterner warning in Matthew 7. Please believe me, I am not judging anyone; certainly, I write these words with the recognition that I am a failed creature, who relies on the blood of Christ to cover my inequities. My words are as much a reminder to myself as I intend them to be for other readers, yet as any good coach should do, I'm saying *now* is the time for some real talk. In Matthew 7:21-23 Jesus says,

> ²¹ Not everyone who says to me, 'Lord, Lord,' will enter the kingdom of heaven, but the one who does the will of my Father who is in heaven. ²² On that day many will say to me, 'Lord, Lord, did we not prophesy in your name, and cast out demons in your name, and do many mighty works in your name?' ²³ And then will I declare to them, 'I never knew you; depart from me, you workers of lawlessness.' Matthew 7:21–23

Here, the Lord is indicating that our proclaimed faith is not enough if we do not back it up with matching works, not being willing to live out the call that God has on our lives (James 2:14-26). Again, I don't want to browbeat you, but this is something you will have to develop with the Lord. It may include holing up daily in a quiet place in a season of prayer to find His will, it may mean taking a step of obedience in an area you already know He has spoken about, or it may mean being the peacemaker in your neighborhood, actively discipling those around you. God knows, and only *you* can find out His will for you.

The bottom line is you simply cannot sit in the stands and allow the race to pass you by. Jesus wants you in it; indeed, He *needs* you in it. The great news is that when you submit to Him, you open yourself up to receive astounding rewards from an extremely loving and generous Creator.

Ask any marathon runner, triathlete, or road racer why they put themselves through the suffering, spent energy, and time it takes to prepare for and complete their races, and you may receive a variety of answers but every single one of their answers will boil down "The Reward." The great runner Steve Prefontaine said,

> You have to wonder at times what you're doing out there. Over the years, I've given myself a thousand reasons to keep running, but it always comes back to where it started. It comes down to self-satisfaction and a sense of achievement.[24]

Others may specify they love the exhilaration of competition, competing against others or against ourselves. For some, the goals may be health-related; they receive a physical benefit by participating. Many competitors train in groups, building tight

---

[24] Jordan, Tom. *Pre: The Story of America's Greatest Running Legend, Steve Prefontaine.* Rodale Books; 2nd edition (March 15, 1997)

relationships with those that they train and suffer with. The benefit in this case is community.

Would you believe when considering one's faith race, the rewards are infinitely greater? In fact, the Bible speaks very clearly about being rewarded for running the race set before us by the Lord. Look at the following five scriptures:

In speaking of Moses leaving a life of luxury and wealth behind, Hebrews 11:26 says, "He considered the reproach of Christ greater wealth than the treasures of Egypt, for he was looking to the reward."

Proverbs 15:6, which is a book of biblical wisdom, says, "In the house of the righteous there is much treasure, but trouble befalls the income of the wicked."

An interesting scripture is 1 Corinthians 9:24: "Do you not know that in a race all the runners run, but only one receives the prize? So run that you may obtain it." This means each of us is to run very competitively in our spiritual race.

I love what Palm 19:9-11 says,

> [9] the fear of the Lord is clean, enduring forever; the rules of the Lord are true, and righteous altogether. [10] More to be desired are they than gold, even much fine gold; sweeter also than honey and drippings of the honeycomb. [11] Moreover, by them is your servant warned; in keeping them there is great reward.

This powerful passage reveals the rewards of Heaven are more like a *source* that generates anything you need, as opposed to physical rewards which are finite and fleeting. Clearly, the fear of the Lord, and the Word of the Lord, bring far more valuable rewards than any earthly treasure.

And last but not least, Philippians 3:13 reminds us of the ultimate reward; one which is great than winning a trillion lotteries in a trillion lifetimes. That is the reward of salvation:

"¹³ Brethren, I do not regard myself as having laid hold of *it* yet; but one thing *I do*: forgetting what *lies* behind and reaching forward to what *lies* ahead, ¹⁴ I press on toward the goal for the prize of the upward call of God in Christ Jesus." (NASB1195)

So we can see from scripture that getting into the race is not only crucial to our relationship with the Lord, but the rewards we will receive are far beyond anything that might tempt us to take priority over God's call. Although it is true we will receive rewards for ourselves in this life, consider as well the profound reward of having an eternal impact on lives that would otherwise be lost in eternity without you getting in the race. Daniel 12:3 tells us of one of Heaven's most powerful and distinguishing rewards, "And those who are wise shall shine like the brightness of the sky above; and those who turn many to righteousness, like the stars forever and ever."

In 2019 Bruce Abbott, Dave Costa, and Gary McBroom (all Malachi Dads volunteers) had just finished breakfast at a local restaurant when, as they were leaving, two men entered the restaurant. One walked straight up to Bruce and said, "You saved my life!"

Bruce was a bit startled but calmly asked with a smile, "How?" The man's stated his name was Aaron and he told Bruce he had been incarcerated at Pitchess Detention Center (South), in Los Angeles County. Aaron had attended the Malachi Dads program where Bruce had taught. Aaron continued that the Malachi Dads program had been the most powerful catalyst and had turned his life completely around. Aaron said he had been sober for five years, and upon his release, he now has a beautiful wife, two precious children, and a good job. The best part was that Aaron had begun participating in programs that allow him to give back and follow Jesus' commandment to "Love your neighbor as yourself" (Mark 12:31). Through Bruce getting into the race, Aaron had learned what it means to be a godly husband, a godly father, and a godly servant.

Aaron gave Bruce the biggest hug and again thanked him profusely.

In March of 2022, at age seventy-four, Bruce Abbott received his eternal reward from his heavenly Father. He had "run" faithfully as a Malachi Dads facilitator for over ten years, leading one of the very first classes in the tough Los Angeles County Jail system. Bruce had a steadfast love for the Lord that was easily seen by all who encountered him. Inmates that knew Bruce felt the love of the living God, and as a result experienced tremendous life-changing hope.

Bruce may not be known to much of the world but who knows what the fruit of his ministry will bring? Could Aaron become the next Billy Graham and lead millions to the Lord? Only the Lord can say, but one thing is for sure … the world would be a much darker place without the work of the Bruce Abbots of the world. Likewise, it will be an immensely brighter place when *you* get in your race.

Conclusion

As I stated at the beginning of this book, I do not claim to offer any great revelation or spiritual insight that others have not laid out before me. My aim is simply to encourage Christians to get off the pew and get into the race. Jesus told us to go into all the world with His message (Matthew 28: 19-20), and the world we occupy is the community in which we live, and our place of work. For those still unsure of how to get into this race Paul speaks of in 2 Timothy 4:7, I want to let you know there are ministries that will assist you with a starting point, and provide you with spiritual and practical support as you grow in your calling.

A large part of my race is run through LGM so I used examples from my experience at LGM to illustrate the point I am making. There are many such ministries you can join when you choose to move from being a spectator in the race to an active participant. The Lord's plan may be for you to travel the world on mission trips but it doesn't mean that is your starting point. Once you make the decision to start running, at whatever pace you choose, the Holy Spirit will be running beside you (actually within you) providing guidance and direction. He may well tell you to dial it up a bit once you begin cruising, but being the excellent coach He is, He will make sure you are equipped for the change.

Having the Lord beside you doesn't mean the enemy won't throw obstacles and challenges in your path, so be prepared to face them head-on and overcome them. Be willing to change course if that is what the Lord directs because it is through change that we grow. Remember, this is as true spiritually as it is physically. We are the long-distance runners Hebrews 12:13 (MSG) is speaking of. Of course, this requires training, endurance, and discipline, if we are not to grow weary and fainthearted (Hebrews 12:3). Paul went through much persecution and suffering in his ministry yet called it a good fight. This is because he knew *why* he was in the fight and never took his eyes off the goal, saying: "So I do not run aimlessly; I do not box as one beating the air" (1 Corinthians 9:26).

General William Booth, the founder of the Salvation Army, modeled remarkable determination and tenacity. In his last speech at a crowded Royal Albert Hall in London, England, he declared,

> While Women weep, as they do now, I'll fight; while children go hungry, as they do now I'll fight; while men go to prison, in and out, in and out, as they do now, I'll fight; while there is a poor lost girl upon the streets, while there remains one dark soul without the light of God, I'll fight, I'll fight to the very end![25]

This is a similar approach to Paul's—no amount of stoning and beatings deterred Paul from his course. If we desire to find our pace, we need to shift our approach from running aimlessly and shadow-boxing to purposefully living out our faith. Fulfilling the specific calling God has for each one of us, however, requires an *intentional* shift in our approach to living out this call. This means a decisive shift in our mindset and priorities.

John Maxwell, the former pastor, speaker, and author of numerous Christian leadership books, articulates this need in his book *Thinking for a Change: 11 Ways Highly Successful People Approach Life and Work*[26]. He points out that for lasting change,

[25] "William Booth's Final Speech Inspiration for New Ad." 2013. Prairie Division. July 4, 2013. https://salvationarmy.ca/prairie/2013/07/william-booths-final-speech-inspiration-for-new-ad/

[26] Maxwell, John C. 2005. Thinking for a Change: 11 Ways Highly Successful People Approach Life and Work. Pg 25. New York: Center Street.

we *must* adjust our way of thinking. By changing our thought processes, Maxwell states you can rise to a "whole new level, personally and professionally." Paul wrote on this subject in his letter to the Romans, a couple of thousand years ago when he said, "Do not be conformed to this world, but be transformed by the renewal of your mind, that by testing you may discern what is the will of God, what is good and acceptable and perfect" (Romans 12:2). Renewing your mind means a deliberate shifting of your thought patterns from putting yourself first to placing a priority on the will of God for your life.

In my experience, many Christians would like to get in the race but are procrastinating for one reason or another. They may be waiting on a "sign" from the Lord or waiting until they "aren't so busy" and have more time for ministry. The reality is God speaks to you primarily through your spirit, in that inner, small voice, and you have to make time for (prioritize) His call. Some, however, just need a gentle push to get them started. This is an opportunity to encourage those around you to join you in the race.

We discussed how it's easier to run a marathon when someone is running with you, so you might have to suggest your church become involved in some sort of ministry program. In doing so you will provide the opportunity for individual members to get off the pews and into the race alongside you, and each other. It is far less daunting to become involved if others are doing it with you, and best of all, you may lead many to righteousness by getting your friends and fellow church members involved, via their ministries.

Suggesting your fellow church members join a program may also be the Lord quickening the pace of *your* ministry. At LGM we engage the localized church or local ministries whenever possible. We do this intentionally as it assists in building a foundation for long-term transformation. Locals on the ground in the community are the most knowledgeable. Indeed, this is where the concept of the apostle came from. There are several easy ways in which a church group can assist in LGM programs. One of these is the Returning Hearts Celebration—an opportunity for incarcerated men and women to engage their children in a safe and fun-filled way.

During the Returning Hearts Celebration, graduates are reunited with their kids—some for the very first time! They get an opportunity to ask for forgiveness, seek reconciliation, and share their love of Christ with their families. The next few hours provide a carnival-like event where parents and kids can get to know each other, begin to build bonds, and set a foundation for positive growth. This treasured day for so many families requires many volunteers to make it a success and is the perfect opportunity for a group from the same church to make a difference in the lives of these families.

Simultaneously, in another area of the facility, as part of the Returning Hearts Celebration, LGM engages the children's guardians. The Guardian Program allows us to share what the students have been learning and what has been a part of their program. It is an opportunity to provide consoling or understanding to guardians who still carry hurt. It also provides the chance to minister to them and engage the guardians in deeper support through their localized church, and possibly encourage the guardians to volunteer in helping facilitate the Malachi Dads or Hannah's Gift programs. My point is look for ways to encourage others to join you; the rewards are varied and plentiful on both sides.

Finally, don't underestimate the value of a mentor, coach, or confidant in your service to the Lord. Having someone to confide in who can also assess your spiritual progress will also not only benefit your life, but you can then learn to teach and become a coach to others. This is what discipling relationships are about— helping others across the finish line.

I urge you to make to decision to get into the race and find your pace, so like Paul, you can say, "I have fought the good fight, I have finished the race," and when you reach the finish line you have single-mindedly focused on throughout your life, you may hear those glorious words "Well done, good and faithful servant!"

Printed in the United States
by Baker & Taylor Publisher Services